BECOMING
A VOICE OF FIRE

A SOUL WITH IMPACT

BECOMING A VOICE OF FIRE

A SOUL WITH IMPACT

DOYL C. TULLY

© 2017 by Doyl Tully. All rights reserved.

Published by Redemption Press, PO Box 427, Enumclaw, WA 98022

Toll Free (844) 2REDEEM (273-3336)

Redemption Press is honored to present this title in partnership with the author. The views expressed or implied in this work are those of the author. Redemption Press provides our imprint seal representing design excellence, creative content, and high quality production.

No part of this publication may be reproduced, stored in a retrieval system, or transmitted in any way by any means—electronic, mechanical, photocopy, recording, or otherwise—without the prior permission of the copyright holder, except as provided by USA copyright law.

All Scripture quotations, unless otherwise indicated, are taken from the New King James Version. Copyright © 1982 by Thomas Nelson, Inc. Used by permission. All rights reserved.

Scripture quotations marked ESV are taken from the Holy Bible, English Standard Version. ESV® Permanent Text Edition® (2016). Copyright © 2001 by Crossway Bibles, a publishing ministry of Good News Publishers.

Scripture quotations marked NASB are taken from the New American Standard Bible® (NASB), Copyright © 1960, 1962, 1963, 1968, 1971, 1972, 1973, 1975, 1977, 1995 by The Lockman Foundation. Used by permission. www.Lockman.org

ISBN 13: 978-1-68314-336-9
978-1-68314-337-6 (ePub)
978-1-68314-338-3 (Mobi)

Library of Congress Catalog Card Number: 2017941205

CONTENTS

1 Introduction...7
2 Fire Components...15
3 Fire Examples...19
4 The Firebox: Demands of a Divine Call.........33
5 The Firebrick: Risky Obedience....................45
6 The Fire Starter: Great Faith........................59
7 The Fire Logs: A Ready Fire Needs Fuel.......71
8 Price: Holy Conduct...................................73
9 Preparation: Being Ready for Success..........83
10 Prayer: The Heart and Soul........................91
11 Perspective: Heavenly Vision....................109
12 Perseverance: Ride the Wave....................119
13 Persistence: Fan the Flame.......................129
14 Conclusion..137

Introduction

IT WAS A BEAUTIFUL, CRISP Sunday morning. I strolled through the front door with my first cup of coffee and out onto the walkway as the sun was shining brightly, and its warmth pressed against my skin. I was on my way to retrieve our newspaper from the front yard as I did each Sunday morning. My whole being was alive; it was Sunday, a day we looked forward to each week as we focused on worship, on God's purpose, and on Him moving in our lives. This Sunday, as was our habit, we would certainly be attending church. It was a great day!

We went about our morning like a well-oiled machine running on all cylinders to accomplish our task of preparing the family for Sunday's service. We had been doing this routine for years; no new ground to cover, but each year or so we added to the size of our family, so the routine only had to be adjusted slightly due to the blessing of children.

Of course, I didn't know that this Sunday would be a serious turning point in the focus and direction of my spiritual life. I didn't have any idea how God would use it to stir my soul—how He would force an explanation of my beliefs, challenge the overall direction of my spiritual voice, and shape a voice after His heart in such a way that many lives would be impacted. I was a Bible study teacher at this time and greatly enjoyed learning, teaching, and applying God's Word. This was the core of who I was in the Lord.

We moved through the morning as usual and enjoyed a powerful time in our Bible study class, teaching His Word, hearing personal testimonies, and sharing ministry opportunities with each other. From there we moved into the worship setting as always, anticipating a time of worship and to be inspired to know Him more.

As background: our church leadership had been moving the church through a cultural change. The pastor had attended a conference about how to become a "seeker style" church. He felt that this ministry approach was a change we needed, and he was leading us to become this kind of church. It was definitely a process of both teaching and trial-and-error implementation. However, the pastor was making progress in his quest to move us in this direction. Changes were common such as writing out your testimony by hand and then going back through it and taking out any references to the blood of Jesus, death on the cross, or the Holy Spirit because it was claimed that these references could be offensive or alarming to seekers. During this transformation time, many didn't fully understand what this new direction meant, but I certainly was willing to allow time and the Holy Spirit to confirm this direction. God always confirms His steps.

This Sunday the worship was outstanding, and I personally worshiped Him deeply. I felt as though Jesus was right there with me, that I might just reach out and touch Him. I felt so moved by the Holy Spirit that His presence brought tears of joy to my eyes. The pastor spoke more about becoming a seeker style church. It was interesting, but something was just not settling into my spirit. It seemed as though each time he spoke on this topic, I had more difficulty connecting the dots with what I knew about God's heartbeat. Let's be clear: I am not saying that he

Introduction

was speaking or leading anyone in a wrong direction. I am just saying that I was having a very difficult time with this seeker-only direction.

At the end of this Sunday's sermon, the pastor told a story. He spoke of a couple who had attended the church last week. They had enjoyed the worship and listened to the message intently. God had moved upon their hearts to such a degree that after the end of the service, the couple came down to the front to speak with him. As a seeker church, we no longer had an altar time for people to respond to the message. The couple communicated that they felt like something was happening inside of them, and they just were not sure what it was. They seemed to be searching for something but didn't come thinking God was what they needed. They continued to express a need for something to help them in life. To me, it was obvious. I thought this was the very hope of every pastor and church who desired to see people like this coming forward to receive Christ as both their Savior and Lord. Right? Instead, he told them he was glad that they felt this way and for them to keep coming back. If God was speaking to them, they would know it in time. What? I just couldn't believe what I was hearing. As believers, we should celebrate this coming forward to seek God. The fact is, we invite, we long, we rejoice when anyone, like this couple, comes forward to say that they are looking for something but are not sure exactly what it is. We say it is Christ Jesus our Lord drawing you by the Holy Spirit. And we then use the opportunity to help them see their need for Christ and lead them to invite Him into their hearts. This pierced me to the soul. I began to question where the voices are today that cry out as one on fire for Christ. Do they exist, or has the church become a casual encounter of people who are indifferent to those whom the Holy Spirit has brought before us? Do voices of fire exist at all?

Today more than ever, both the world and the church are in need of what I call voices of fire, voices who hear from God and speak the truth in a culture that's revealing a desperate need for it, voices for the Lord who will not dull the cutting edge on the sword of God's truth, voices who believe and preach, teach and live all of God's Word regardless of the way it is received or the way it makes one feel. Where are these voices today? Where are the voices who are willing to step out by the movement of the Holy Spirit within their souls, willing to speak a message from God, willing to take risky steps of obedience to the King, willing to be considered foolish by the world, willing to speak without compromise, and willing to speak with conviction, with power, with authority, with wisdom, and with God's revealed truth.

I see a church culture that is sacrificing voices of fire for voices of crowd pleasers, voices of power-of-positive-speech, and voices who are careful to not offend anyone. I constantly run into voices who seem more concerned about building impressive ministries, imposing buildings, bank accounts, and projecting images of church success as the world sees it rather than voices who consist of fervent, fiery communication of the gospel of Jesus Christ. I see a body of Christ that is impressed with size, success as man defines it, and everything grand in size instead of being impressed with the power of God that moves though voices who hear from God, voices God uses to impact lives each and every day.

I believe the heart of God is grieved by our lack of salt and our unwillingness to speak the whole truth. The church today is losing, if it has not already lost, its savor and will someday soon be rendered powerless in a world that is in need of a message from men and women who are voices of fire. I am disturbed by how many leaders are embracing this approach of preaching the Word of God. It is understandable that the sheep follow and enjoy this style of teaching, but it is inexcusable for godly leaders to pursue a man-pleasing approach any more.

Now, let me be clear about who a voice of fire is. They are not loud, passionate speakers who hurl judgment at sinners. They are not men who preach down to people trying to make them feel guilty in order to get a response. They are not men who purposely beat up people with

God's Word and somehow receive personal gratification from it. This is *not* what I mean by voices of fire. The voices of fire I am referring to are men and women who know God, love Jesus Christ, have a desire for all to hear the truth of God's Word in completeness, and stand ready to walk in His revealed truth. Yes, they preach, teach, and live with passion, they preach and teach the whole Word of God, and they know Him and His ways intimately. They are men and women who have spent time with God, know Him, and communicate His heart for the people with power! Voices of fire are people who preach and teach and live a life of power.

We have many examples of voices of fire in God's Word. Let me share with you a few men who are great examples of voices of fire. It is important for you to understand the type of person I am talking about.

Examples

A man like Abraham who lived his life with such faith in God that, "it was accounted to him as righteousness" (Rom. 4:3 ESV). This life was a voice of fire to such a degree that Hebrews tells us he believed God could bring Isaac back from the dead. This had never been considered up to this point in Scripture by anyone. Abraham believed God, lived His faith to the extreme, and stood for truth. Certainly a voice of fire!

A man like David who proclaimed awesome truths of God through the Scripture in some of the most difficult circumstances. He passionately knew our Lord in such a way that God proclaimed him, "A man after my own heart" (Acts 13:22). Certainly a voice of fire!

A man like Nehemiah who led with such wisdom and truth that God used him to rebuild the wall of Jerusalem, something that had not been done for one hundred fifty years. A man who took a huge risk of losing his life in coming before the king in order to become what God was shaping him to be. Certainly a voice of fire!

A man like Elijah who stood before a king and proclaimed the judgment of the Most High God without fear when his life was on the line. He also stood before the priests of Baal and the people, calling fire from heaven to consume the sacrifice prepared unto the Lord revealing who was the one and only true God, "The Lord, He is God; the Lord, He is God" (1 Kings 18:39 ESV). Certainly a voice of fire!

A man like John the Baptist who was a voice strongly crying out about our coming Savior and being used of God to make ready the way of the Lord. His message was both powerful and so full of substance that people flocked to hear him and then responded with repentance and baptism. He was faithful to his call, ministered about six months to one year, and was beheaded. Certainly a voice of fire who fulfilled his part in the revealing grace of God!

> I indeed baptize you with water unto repentance, but He who is coming after me is mightier than I, whose sandals I am not worthy to carry. He will baptize you with the Holy Spirit and fire. (Matt. 3:11)

A man like Peter, who was a nobody from a very small fishing community. After being confronted with the living, loving Savior of the world, he committed his life, heart and soul, to proclaiming the name of our Lord Jesus Christ. At Pentecost, while moved by the Holy Spirit, he revealed truth with such power that about three thousand souls were saved as a result of his sermon. Certainly a voice of fire!

> Therefore let all the house of Israel know assuredly that God has made this Jesus, whom you crucified. (Acts 2:36)

A man like Paul who was known as the worst of the worst. He was viewed by many as a murderer, certainly a Christian hater, and a legalist with a passion to punish even to the point of death any who would break his rules. He would certainly not be a great candidate to be used in the kingdom, right? *Not!* Jesus met him face-to-face on the road to Damascus one day and turned his heart one hundred and eighty degrees. He became a man who burned so brightly that the only way to silence him was to kill him. Paul himself proclaimed:

> I have been crucified with Christ; it is no longer I who live, but Christ lives in me; and the life which I now live in the flesh I live by faith in the Son of God, who loved me and gave Himself for me. (Gal. 2:20)

Certainly a voice of fire!

All of these men were voices of fire. Of course, there are many others we read about in the Scriptures and those that we know not: common, every day men and women who were nothing without Christ, but with Christ all things became possible. Men and women with voices of fire and godly character who can teach us by their examples: all being called of God, undeniably chosen by the King, full of boldness and faith, preaching the truth at all costs, and calling sin, sin. All of these voices of fire were positioned in the right place at the right time, living life with holy conduct, willing to give instant obedience, selfless in all things—men and women this world was not worthy of, but they were called to be voices of fire! We see fire from heaven arriving on the scene because these men and women of God were called, found faithfully moving in obedience to His will, and believing Him in the face of absolute evil.

Know this for sure: *It is absolutely crucial for anyone desiring to become a voice of fire to be called of God and know this calling without any shadow of a doubt!*

Without knowing this call, you will be ripped apart without mercy, shredded, spit out, scoffed as fake, and in all probability, become a quitter. In other words, you will not succeed in the full destiny and purpose in that which God has called you. This is not to say you will lose your salvation or have no rewards in heaven. Of course, you will. That is not what this book is about. It is about becoming a voice who is strong and unwavering, bold yet trained, and both powerful and compassionate, sharing the truths of God—true voices who are being used for the Lord God Almighty for His purpose and pleasure. I promise you this: you will need to return to this defining moment of the call of God often because this life God has called you to, becoming a voice of fire, is both life's greatest joy and greatest suffering.

Are you willing to follow? Are you willing to become a voice of fire? Then keep reading and allow the Holy Spirit to work within your heart, and I am fully convinced you can become His voice of fire for today!

2

Fire Components

I GREW UP ON THE Pacific coast along the northern coastline of California. I lived in a very small fishing and logging town about twenty miles south of the Oregon border. I was fortunate enough to live one mile from the Pacific Ocean and one mile from the great redwood forests. It was an amazing place to grow up. I remember riding my bike to the ocean, the mountains, and into the redwood forest.

My dad worked in the lumber industry. We, a family of five, lived in a small house by today's standards but very adequate for our family. The three boys slept in one bedroom, and mom and dad had their bedroom. There was a single bathroom that serviced the family, a small kitchen/dining area, and a living area. In this part of the country, we heated our house using a floor furnace. On cold days, we would all gather early at the furnace to get the best warmth as it bellowed out its heated air.

As far back as I can remember, my dad had a dream of having a large fireplace for our home. He would often talk about how great it would be for us. I remember him talking about its great benefits. He declared it would produce ten times more heat than our old floor furnace. "It, for sure, would heat most of the house," he said. Then he would begin talking about how he could build it. He would carefully prepare all aspects of the fireplace from the fixed box to the finishing touches. His dream was a white limestone exterior. He always told me that, by design, each component of the fireplace was very important because it was necessary to harness the fire to heat our home. I remember he also stressed the importance of the fireplace draw. He was referring to how the fire would draw oxygen to itself so that it would continue to burn. Without this, he would say, "The fire would go out! And we wouldn't want that, would we?" He was so right; we wouldn't want the fire to go out. My dad finally built his fireplace, and it was grand. So, how you build the fireplace, a place prepared to host the fire itself, is very important. So let's look at how we should prepare for the place of the fire in our lives.

It is important for me to be very clear about how a voice of fire burns, how it will be most productive while burning, and what keeps it from burning out of control and being destructive. We all understand that a fire with no boundaries will become a wildfire and consume everything in its path. This is not what we desire. We should desire a fire that is created inside of us by the Holy Spirit, allowing for light, protection, comfort, warmth, safety, and direction for all who come. This is what a voice of fire will be. God even placed our tongue, which can be a "fire" in and of itself, inside a box to control it—it is called your mouth. Likewise, a fire must be placed inside a firebox to be sure it has a controlled burn. In our case, we must have a Holy Spirit controlled burn. A perfect burn is controlled by God, the Holy Spirit!

Therefore, the idea of the fire components is simple, purposeful, and useful for this analogy. Its creator has designed it to contain, control, build, and focus the fire to make sure it burns as hot as possible while also controlling its burn and thus providing its fullest potential. This design allows for the fire's maximum purpose:

Fire Components

- Light in the darkness
- Protection from cold
- Comfort by its presence
- Warmth from the cold and damp
- Heat source for cooking
- Safety from attacks

Using the fire to its fullest potential brings so much to its user. However, in order for a fire to be burned in this way, all of the components must be properly created and maintained. Otherwise, we could have an out-of-control fire causing nothing but total destruction; a fire with no containment is a wildfire of total devastation. Fire is very dangerous, and we must have a place for this fire to produce maximum benefits. Thus, our greatest need is a location for the fire and all the components necessary to start and keep it burning. These things must be in place prior to the starting the fire. In many homes and other structures, a firebox is used to contain the fire.

I know you are not that interested in the technical components of a fireplace, but it is vital for the balance of this book and, therefore, is very needful and useful for us to quickly cover this explanation. Let me say here, I am not trying in any way to suggest that you could build a real fire or fireplace from this description, but it will help you understand more in the next chapters and allows me to use it as an analogy for the rest of our development of the topic.

Let's quickly look at the four fire components necessary for a fire to burn at maximum potential. I will use these components and discuss them as they relate to becoming a voice of fire throughout this book. Allow me to briefly introduce and simply discuss these four components.

Four Components of a Fire

1. Firebox. This is commonly a three-sided box of fireproof, heavy-gauged metal that protects the outer elements of the fireplace. It is the framework in which the fire resides. It is designed to focus the fire in a single direction by producing a blocking layer on three sides. The outside layer guarantees the fire will not burn in an unwanted direction. The firebox is the place in which the rest of the components are built.

2. Firebrick. These bricks are specially fired, can withstand high temperatures, and are designed to repel heat into the opposite direction. They are very important for the overall success of the purpose of a fire. They are laid in the bottom and line the sides. So, by design, these bricks withstand the intense heat and repel it through the front of the firebox.

3. Fire Starter. These are specially selected small pieces of wood, called kindling that are dry and ready for a spark to ignite them. By design, this material is so dry and combustible that the least spark will cause it to burst into flames, creating the genesis for a continuing blaze.

4. Fire Logs. This component cannot be ignored. While the fire starter will begin the blaze, only the fire logs will keep it going and growing to the most powerful blaze possible. These logs are especially selected for size, type, and weight in order to produce the best, hottest, and longest burning fire.

In chapter four, I will use these components as an analogy on how voices of fire should be equipped and prepared. I believe this will help your understanding as I develop each of these topics.

3

Fire Examples

IT IS VERY COMMON TO see fire and God moving through the Scriptures. We see holy fire providing the avenue for revelation from God, protection of His people, leading for His people, judgment for the world and our works, and deliverance of man. We also see that fire is used in the description of the Lord's eyes in Revelation: "They were like a flame of fire" (Rev 2:18 ESV). Let us not forget that the fire of God placed within someone by the call of God on their heart will set a person ablaze yet not burn them up! Of course, it makes perfect sense that we should become voices of fire when there is a fire burning within us.

Typically, God uses fire in two ways to describe His truths. One is judgment. The second is His revelation. Revelation is the focus here. Let's look at a few examples of how fire was used to communicate to man and through man.

Example 1: Fire Reveals God's Commands

After forty years of a mundane life of meditation and communion, Moses saw God manifest Himself through fire. Exodus 3:2 says, "And the Angel of the Lord appeared to him in a flame of fire from the midst of a bush. So he looked, and behold, the bush was burning with fire, but the bush was not consumed."

One of the good things about God revealing Himself to His servant through fire was that he didn't have to worry about it burning him up! The second thing is that God gave Moses a direct revelation to act upon. It was literally a fiery manifestation of God communicating to Moses what God had in mind for him to do.

I want you to notice two things about this manifestation of God through fire that have direct application for us today.

God Manifests Himself to the Faithful

Moses existed on the back side of the desert for some forty years as he learned important truths about God's timing. It would have been easy for him to say, "I am done trying to serve God." He could have said, "I have had enough" and then just slipped into a depressed heart, feeling worthless. Yet, during this time of waiting, it was not like Moses was sitting around doing nothing or freeloading from his father-in-law, Jethro. Not at all. Moses remained industrious and engaged in the honorable work of tending to the flock of Jethro, humble as that may have been. The point is that God reveals Himself to those who can be found keeping their flocks, those who are found faithful in doing honorable things. Being found faithful is key!

God is pleased when He finds us at work. At this point, Moses was not a man of power or fame. He was a man of total insignificance. We find him here in a lowly position, shepherding a flock of sheep that were not even his own. However, that was no problem for God. You do not need to have position in this world to be of service to God. Earthly position is not a qualification for God's service, but faithfulness and character are very much God's qualifications for kingdom work.

Fire Examples

God Manifests Himself through Fire

On Mount Horeb, God manifested Himself to Moses using a burning bush, a thorny shrub, and not some kind of majestic tree or any other magnificent thing. He chose a lowly thorn bush to give clear revelation to Moses. Look at Exodus 3:2–3.

> And the Angel of the Lord appeared to him in a flame of fire from the midst of a bush. So he looked, and behold, the bush was burning with fire, but the bush was not consumed. Then Moses said, "I will now turn aside and see this great sight, why the bush does not burn."

This was not some kind of fire that man can make but a fire that only God can create; it was a blaze that was able to burn but not destroy. This was a fire that had a purpose and reason for existence. It was a fire that would get our attention. That was exactly what happened to Moses; he stopped and realized that this was something very unusual, and that he must pay attention. The fire of God must also get our attention. We must be able to recognize it, stop, and seek His revelation, taking the time to see Him. Moses turned to look and see. Stopping and taking the time to look and see is when we will recognize the full revelation of God. Stopping to take time for God is the beginning of receiving revelation.

What we see in this setting is a revelation through fire. This fire represents the presence of God—the holiness and the glory of God. God reveals Himself through it, allowing Moses to know more about his purpose. *My friend, knowing God is a prerequisite for becoming a voice of fire.* The better we know Him, the more willing we are to be found faithful, increasing the revelation in our lives and thus creating a stronger voice for Him.

Are you ready to receive a revelation from God, to stand in the very center of His presence, holiness, and glory? Are you moving each day in a way that seeks to know Him more? Are you declaring daily your full dependence and reliance on Him and remaining busy about your given tasks, faithfully serving Him? If you are, His revelation will come. I declare over you: *You will become a voice of fire!*

Example 2: Fire Leads the Way

God clearly directs His people by fire. This story is about God leading the children of Israel in the wilderness by fire at night. There is no question that God is directing their path, and it is illuminated, directed, and warmed by holy fire! Without the fire by night, His people would have been stopped dead in their tracks. This is the main problem with the Christian churches today: a lack of fire in leading the congregations. This is why we find psychological manipulation, mere motivational speakers, and unqualified perversion holding places of honor within what is called the body of Christ. Where there is no holy fire, there is no direction. *God's people have lost their way in the darkness and allowed feel-good messengers to guide them instead of His holy fire.* Here we see:

God Led His People with a Pillar of Fire

> And the Lord went before them by day in a pillar of cloud to lead the way, and by night in a pillar of fire to give them light, so as to go by day and night. He did not take away the pillar of cloud by day or the pillar of fire by night from before the people. (Ex. 13:21–22)

I believe it was the Holy Spirit leading here, manifested in the form of fire. There is a very strong resemblance between this fire and the Holy Spirit in our lives today. The One leading us through our Christian life is the Holy Spirit, guiding, revealing, comforting, and giving us confidence to move even through the darkness. Let's look at the four likenesses of the pillar of fire and the Holy Spirit.

Fire Examples

1. The Pillar of Fire Was a Gift from God

This is another magnificent manifestation of His grace. His people did nothing to deserve Him, earn Him, or even work for Him. God just poured out His wonderful grace through His guidance by night through the pillar of fire. In the same way, to the believer, the Holy Spirit is a gift of God.

> And I will pray the Father, and He will give you another Helper, that He may abide with you forever. (John 14:16)

2. The Pillar of Fire Had a Purpose

This pillar of fire was not just some random act of God to impress His children. It was not some kind of magic act to amuse us. There were very specific purposes for this pillar of fire. It was there to lead them in the way they should go, to give light, and to demonstrate the power and presence of their God!

> For as many as are led by the Spirit of God, these are sons of God. (Rom. 8:14)

> However, when He, the Spirit of truth, has come, He will guide you into all truth; for He will not speak on His own authority, but whatever He hears He will speak; and He will tell you things to come. (John 16:13)

The Bible says that His children will be led by the Spirit of God, and He will guide them into all truth. Wow! What a wonderful passage. Just as the pillar of fire led His children in the darkness of night, we, too, have the Holy Spirit to lead us through darkness, man's reasoning, and doubt into all truth. It's by this fire that we live in the light!

3. The Pillar of Fire Had Protection

Protection is something on which we spend a great deal of time, thought, concern, and money to make sure we are safe. The US spends billions of dollars on our defense systems to make sure that we are as safe as possible as a nation. We place deadbolts on our doors, install security systems in our homes, own watchdogs, and some even purchase firearms to feel as safe as possible. Let me just come out and say this: You are not safe in this world by the devices of man! Our only safety comes by a personal relationship with the Father though Jesus Christ and the Holy Spirit present now, living in us, and protecting our every step. The Bible even goes so far as to say that the steps of the righteous are ordered by the Lord. Think about this: God is caring and ordering our every step. My friend, that is protection!

> And do not grieve the Holy Spirit of God, by whom you were sealed for the day of redemption. (Eph. 4:30)

4. The Pillar of Fire Had Permanence

Have you ever asked yourself why the pillar of fire did not go out? It was there every night, seven nights a week, on and on and on! God appointed it to be there permanently until His purpose for it was accomplished. We, too, have the permanence of the Holy Spirit to be with us as a helper until we shall see Him and then forever.

> And I will pray the Father, and He will give you another Helper, that He may abide with you forever. (John 14:16)

Oh, how we need the fire of the Holy Spirit to lead the way for God's church today. Will you allow your voice to be used to proclaim truth?

Fire Examples

This voice of fire must prevail. Know that God will use this voice to reveal His path! If so, I declare over you: *You will become a voice of fire!*

Example 3: Fire Consumes Our Sacrifice

Here we consider fire from heaven. This is one of the most powerful examples of how God responds to His servants as they place their faith completely in Him and are aligned with His purpose. In this case, Elijah challenged the prophets of Baal to a "real god" test. His purpose was to convince the people that there was only one true God, Jehovah. The way Elijah chose to play out this duel was through the act of worship. I think this was the most amazing and powerful way to demonstrate the real god. Surely the real God would respond to His prophets in worship, right? Well, as you know, the one true God did with absoluteness and power. God responded with fire from heaven as His servant Elijah worshiped.

It is also interesting what James says about this man called Elijah:

> Elijah was a man with a nature like ours, and he prayed earnestly that it would not rain; and it did not rain on the land for three years and six months. And he prayed again, and the heaven gave rain, and the earth produced its fruit. (James 5:17–18)

Clearly, the Bible is saying that Elijah was just a normal person like you, and yet he called fire down from heaven! Regular people like you and I can be used by our God to fulfill His purpose on this earth, even if it means calling fire down from heaven.

I want us to look at the five requirements to see fire from heaven.

1. We Must Prepare the Place of Worship

> Then Elijah said to all the people, "Come near to me." So all the people came near to him. And he repaired the altar of the Lord that was broken

> down. And Elijah took twelve stones, according to the number of the tribes of the sons of Jacob, to whom the word of the Lord had come, saying, "Israel shall be your name." Then with the stones he built an altar in the name of the Lord; and he made a trench around the altar large enough to hold two seahs of seed. (1 Kings 18:30–32)

Elijah needed to create a place of worship so that all could see the power and realness of His God. He created an altar on which to place his sacrifice and as a place to call upon His God. Here was his place to commune with God, to have fellowship with Him. In other words, he built an altar in the name of the Lord God.

Just like Elijah, we must have a place of worship, a place to come and seek the fire of God, to commune, to ask, to seek, to find. This is for both individual and corporate worship. We all must find that place individually so we can seek the Lord with passion, weeping, concern, and to hear His voice. During our commutes to and from work is not what I am talking about here. There must be a place set aside that you make special time to spend with the Father. Also, God calls us to worship corporately, promising us that He will be in our midst as we come together to worship Him. Who, being a child of the Most High, would not want to be where Jesus is? Find your church and go regularly!

2. We Must Be Ready to Sacrifice to Worship

> And he put the wood in order, cut the bull in pieces, and laid it on the wood. (1 Kings 18:33)

Elijah created an altar to place his sacrifice upon as an offering unto the Lord. This particular offering was called a sin offering. Elijah was interceding for the sinfulness of Israel and asking for mercy for all through this sacrifice. Elijah, a voice of fire, understood the root problem—sin.

A voice of fire must be ready to sacrifice in order to worship God, to intercede for others, and to ask God for great mercy for our sins. This is the right answer for many of the problems we face today. Sin has caused a major insensitivity to things of God and will continue to erode our voices and commitment. Sin is our problem and God's mercy is desperately needed to forgive our people and heal our land! *If voices of fire will not proclaim this message, then from where shall it come?*

3. We Must Believe for the Power of God to Come

> "Fill four water pots with water, and pour it on the burnt sacrifice and on the wood." Then he said, "Do it a second time," and they did it a second time; and he said, "Do it a third time," and they did it a third time. So the water ran all around the altar; and he also filled the trench with water. (1 Kings 18:33b–35)

His next step revealed the intimacy and confidence with which Elijah acted. He filled four barrels with water and poured it on the altar once, twice, three times, until the altar and sacrifice were dripping wet, and the water flowed into a trench around the altar. In other words, it was saturated with water. He was crazy! Who can start a fire with wet wood? Burning wet wood is almost impossible, but my friend, God can!

Here is one of the greatest demonstrations of the power of God before our eyes, and He used a normal man to reveal it. Voices of fire are people of faith who can believe God to start fires when the sacrifice, wood, altar, etc. are completely saturated with the very substance that would normally put out the fire. Think about this.

God sometimes allows lives to be drenched and saturated with impossibilities before He moves in power. Our great difficulties become the canvas of triumph for God's glory to be shown. Voices of fire understand, believe, and look for God's fire from heaven even when things and lives are saturated with impossibilities!

4. We Must Engage in Fervent Prayer

> And it came to pass, at the time of the offering of the evening sacrifice, that Elijah the prophet came near and said, "Lord God of Abraham, Isaac, and Israel, let it be known this day that You are God in Israel and I am Your servant, and that I have done all these things at Your word. Hear me, O Lord, hear me, that this people may know that You are the Lord God, and that You have turned their hearts back to You again." (1 Kings 18:36–37)

It seems asking God to move in the impossible is almost unheard of today, and many people pursue all other possible solutions without fervently asking God for "fire from heaven."

Elijah prayed for the glory of God to be revealed. Elijah prayed for his own testimony to be validated. Elijah prayed for the exalting of God's Word. Elijah prayed for a revival among the people. Elijah fervently prayed that God would move and create a fire, not for show, but to put His glory and power on display.

Notice that fervent prayer does not necessarily equal long, drawn-out praying. This prayer of Elijah was both effective and fervent. It reached out with direct, to-the-point asking of God! No need for Elijah to try to impress God with His words or knowledge of the Scriptures. No lessons in how much Elijah knows of God, just a clear and direct prayer communicated in just a few sentences.

Understand this: *The results of our effective prayers today are found not in the moment of needing prayer, but rather is a direct link to the faithfulness of our pursuit of God in the past!*

5. We Must Desire Fire for the Right Reason

> Hear me, O Lord, hear me, that this people may know that You are the Lord God, and that You have turned their hearts back to You again. (1 Kings 18:37)

Elijah asked for the right reason. His only desire was that the hearts of the people would turn back to the Lord God Almighty.

Voices of fire must keep focused for the right reason. We must never make God into a show or adopt some kind of name-it-and-claim-it mindset. We must always keep focused on the real need and ask God to work on our behalf, having mercy on our souls.

What was the result? Fire from heaven that consumed the sacrifice!

> Then the fire of the Lord fell and consumed the burnt sacrifice, and the wood and the stones and the dust, and it licked up the water that was in the trench. Now when all the people saw it, they fell on their faces; and they said, "The Lord, He is God! The Lord, He is God!" (1 Kings 18:38–39)

Fire fell from heaven in abundance, consuming everything: the sacrifice, wood, stones, dust, and even the water. This is one of the greatest demonstrations of the power of God in all of Scripture. Be sure and notice that the fire fell on the altar not the people! The people deserved it, but Elijah interceded, God had mercy, and the people were saved. What an amazing voice of fire, totally interceding for all the people, and God used Elijah for this purpose!

It is crucial for the church today to see voices of fire rise up and take this wonderful lead. God is looking for voices of fire just like Elijah today. We should be using these examples to give us sure footing and a strong voice, a voice of fire to intercede for all people. The Bible says that Elijah was a man with a nature like ours! Are you willing and ready to be an Elijah? If so, I declare over you: *You will become a voice of fire!*

Now, this all leads us to the New Testament where we find the essence of becoming a voice of fire. All we are in the Lord must be grounded and rooted in His revelation to us. This passage is where we find one of the most amazing truths for us today. Paul proclaims:

> Therefore, since we are receiving a kingdom which cannot be shaken, let us have grace, by which we may serve God acceptably with reverence and godly fear. For our God is a consuming fire. (Heb. 12:28–29)

Much is revealed in this verse, but let me just quickly look at the very nature of God in every believer. First, as believers, we receive a kingdom which cannot be shaken. This again reveals that what belongs to us through Christ Jesus our Lord, cannot be torn down, moved away, taken away, or shaken in any way! Get this: we have received something that no attack of the enemy, no circumstance in which we find ourselves, no bad happening, no insult, and no relationship known to mankind can in any way change our position in God's great kingdom. I am secure in His kingdom forever!

Second, we are to express our unwavering gratitude to God. As we realize the depth of our position in His kingdom and that nothing can ever shake us from it, we are overcome by humbling, heartfelt gratitude to God.

Third, we are so moved by His blessings that we offer Him all of who we are in service to His kingdom with a sense of reverence and awe that we are a part of that kingdom.

Fourth, all of this is revealed and manifested because our God is a consuming fire. There it is!

How can we become a voice of fire? From where would the genesis of this fire come? How can we be sure our voices will be of truth and revelation? Our God is a consuming fire. This is our burning bush, much like Moses' burning bush experience when God spoke, yet the bush was not destroyed. God gave Moses signs, commands, truth, and direction. Like Moses' burning bush, the Holy Spirit consumes us with His fire, yet does not destroy us. This is the essence of our fire and revelation, the fountain from where our voice of fire comes! Without the fire of the Holy Spirit in us, no voice of fire exists!

Fire Examples

We see this manifested at Pentecost as the Holy Spirit was given to the disciples in the upper room.

> And suddenly there came a sound from heaven, as of a rushing mighty wind, and it filled the whole house where they were sitting. Then there appeared to them divided tongues, as of fire, and one sat upon each of them. And they were all filled with the Holy Spirit and began to speak with other tongues, as the Spirit gave them utterance. (Acts 2:2–4)

This gives additional meaning to the Pentecost passage, "tongues, as of fire, and one sat upon each of them" because the Holy Spirit was sent visibly to the believers in the upper room revealed in tongues of fire, which resulted not in more prayers, but each believer becoming a voice of fire. It is God's desire for us to become a voice of fire through the Holy Spirit who proclaims the gospel of Jesus Christ: that He died, was buried, and was raised from the dead all for the forgiveness of sins. Peter said:

> Repent, and let every one of you be baptized in the name of Jesus Christ for the remission of sins; and you shall receive the gift of the Holy Spirit. (Acts 2:38)

It is the very heartbeat of God for us to be simply used by the Holy Spirit to speak with fire—to be men and women who possess fire from the Holy Spirit and knowing Him, His heartbeat, His ways, speaking truth, and yes, even experiencing tongues of fire as vessels of truth for His kingdom. This, truly, is not complex or difficult at all. We just permit the Holy Spirit to come upon us and allow God to demonstrate His power through us.

Keep in mind that there is a huge difference between a voice of fire (truth) and a voice of compromise or a voice masked in something that just makes us feel good. Today, we find so many voices saying everything is good. The truth is we are sinful and ungodly in our flesh and need to hear a message of truth to remind us to repent and move again in the steps of God. He desires us to search His Word, to study to understand Him and His heart, to pray for revelation, to give without bounds, to assemble with other believers who long for His presence, to seek ways to actively serve Him, and above all, to share Christ with everyone! If these things are not present in your life, you will never become a voice of fire. If they are, I declare over you: *You will become a voice of fire!*

The Firebox: Demands of a Divine Call

IN NOVEMBER 1992, WE ARRIVED on a Sunday morning at our old home church from years past. We began this quasi-reunion by attending our beloved Bible study class. I was un-expectantly asked if I would share what God was doing in our lives. Of course, I love to take any opportunity to tell people what my great God has done for me. The leaders touched base with other classes to see if they would like to participate in our coming together.

It was a good time. People's lives were touched, and the Holy Spirit was powerfully present. I was thankful for this, and the people voiced their appreciation for my sharing. Now it was time for us to move into the worship service.

I was busy fellowshipping and almost late for the starting hymn but quickly sat down beside my beautiful wife. We settled in among the three hundred or so people for what I had hoped to be a time spent with Jesus Christ through the power of His Spirit.

The service started in an older, traditional style by singing hymns and, of course, the collection of offerings. We were currently members of a contemporary style church in another state, so it was good to sing the old hymns, and I worshiped the Lord through them. I enjoyed the deep reflection and strong theology that each hymn seemed to sing out. I had no idea what was about to happen.

The speaker stood and began the message. After about five minutes, I was getting frustrated. He was not making sense to me. He seemed to be unprepared. The message didn't appear to be going anywhere that would impact my walk in Christ, and there was no power from the Most High.

I was not very happy. I wanted more that day. I wanted a hot word from God straight from the throne room right into my heart—one that would challenge me, motivate me, move me off dead center; one that I could shout out, "Amen!" You know, a real barn burner.

I began to tune the speaker out and chew on the Lord's ear. I asked Him, What was going on here? These people needed to hear the pure Word of God, something that will move them and help them grow in Him. I was really getting into it and complaining in my spirit.

When I finally stopped to take a breath, the Lord spoke to me. Now, God had spoken to me many times in a variety of ways, but to this point in my walk with Christ, He had spoken only a very few times. However, God spoke into my mind and heart, and this is what He said: "Doyl, this is what I want you to do. I want you to preach the Word of God to people just like these." What? Lord, could you repeat that please? Nothing. I heard it right!

I was staggered! Needless to say, I did not hear another word from the speaker. I sat in a stunned state of mind I could not shake. My mind exploded with reasons that this command was ridiculous. I could never preach the Word like a preacher or pastor. I couldn't because of many reasons. I couldn't because I had issues. I couldn't because I had no training. I couldn't because I was too old to start that kind of journey. I couldn't because I had a wife and three children. I couldn't because I had a wonderful job and career. Then I stopped. I told my mind to be quiet. I took a deep breath. This was an amazing call of God on my life!

The Firebox: Demands of a Divine Call

The loving, living God Almighty had called me to preach His Word and all that is required with this calling.

I will remember that day for the rest of my life, and I share this call on my life so as to be very clear. *The only thing that can be your firebox is the call of God on your life.* It forms the fire box that will guarantee that the fire will burn and remain directed in the appropriate direction, allowing for maximum fire purpose. It is made of very thick skin, meant to be impenetrable—a real line in the sand that even the hordes of evil or the gates of hell cannot break through. As difficulties, trials, and evil try to stop your purpose, you will need to return to the surety of the firebox. *We are called of God!* Nothing can stop a man or woman who has this firebox in place and truly believes that it is so.

So, let me share this truth: *The call of God on your life summons you to your divine destiny.*

For a voice of fire to exist, the call of God is a must-have. This is a requirement, not an option. There must be a time in your life that you heard the call of God, His revelation, and you know that this is of the Father. You are moved and compelled by His call and will find yourself seeking steps to realize the fullness of the call of God.

I have discovered three foundational truths about this call of God. These truths have helped bring clarity and intensity to my calling.

1. As Believers, We Are All Called

There are two types of calls I am referring to in this truth. There exists a *general call* to all who will believe.

> But you are *a chosen race*, a royal *priesthood, a holy nation, a people for* his *own possession*, that you may proclaim the excellencies of him *who has called you* out of darkness into His marvelous light. (1 Peter 2:9 ESV, emphasis added)

This is the general call of God to each and every believer to accept Jesus Christ as their Savior and Lord and to move out of darkness into His marvelous light. This is the call from the Holy Spirit on each person who will receive this wonderful salvation. Once we respond to this call, we find ourselves residing in His marvelous light, able to know, seek, realize, respond, and experience the joy of our relationship in Christ. Please, speak this truth out loud as though it is real: "*I am called of God!*"

There is also a *specific call* of God for each believer as they find themselves in Christ. Take note of the specific call that was given to Saul (Paul) and Barnabas:

> And while they were ministering to the Lord and fasting, the Holy Spirit said, "Set apart for me Barnabas and Saul for the work to which I have called them." (Acts 13:2 ESV)

This is the call of God that the Holy Spirit specifically places in your heart so that you might hear, know, and obey in order to accomplish the specific work and purpose that God has for you. Many times, this shows up in your heart one day and somehow you just know that you must do a specific ministry, work, or task for the Lord. Or the Holy Spirit impresses directly on your heart the calling into a specific ministry. This results in you knowing you have heard the voice of God or that God has placed a yearning in your heart to be engaged on this earth for His kingdom with your specific task.

Please, speak this truth out loud as though it is real: "*I am called of God!*"

2. We Are All Called Out

All believers are called out of darkness, the previous life, the attachment of things, ungodly relationships, the pull of this world, and the self-promoting acts into His marvelous purpose, plan, and destiny with a full dependency on Him for their lives.

The Bible clearly beckons us in this way:

"Therefore, *come out from their midst and be separate*," says the Lord. (2 Cor. 6:17 emphasis added)

Come out of this world into the land of promise I have for you says the Lord. Separate yourself unto Christ and enter into your destiny, one of significance and purpose for His kingdom.

Please, speak this truth out loud as though it is real: *"I am called of God!"*

3. We Are All Called to Go

Whether you understand the destination or details of the call or not, is not the main issue. We are called to go!

This leads me to the next powerful truth: *Many times, we don't know exactly where we are going.*

At times, God just gives us the high-level call, says *go*, and we are to obey Him, trusting that at the right time, God will reveal more of His purpose and plan. This is a very challenging time because you are moving with very little revelation, but you must obey the call, and nothing less will be accepted by our Lord.

Please, speak this truth out loud as though it is real: *"I am called of God!"*

Now that we have strongly established the call of God and that we are all called, there is something more that must be realized. So many just leave it here: Yes, we are called. Yes, we are called out. Yes, we are called to go! Sounds good, right? But before we leave this powerful truth, there are more revelations that must be brought forward. It is what I call:

The Four Demands of a Divine Call

It is the lack of understanding four simple but powerful truths that keep so many Christians from realizing their destiny in Christ. Let's look at them one at a time.

1. We Must Expect Separation

> Now the Lord had said to Abram: "Get out of your country, from your family and from your father's house." (Gen. 12:1a)

The context of this verse is that Abram was living quietly in the outskirts of Ur, worshiping pagan gods, surrounded by evil, and ignoring the very existence of God, the one, true God. Then suddenly, the God of glory appeared to him and called him out. It was a marvelous appearance. What did God say? God simply instructed Abram to depart from where he was living. He was to leave his land, his relatives, and his father's house. This was a definite call of separation. God commanded Abram to separate himself from all the people, family, and possessions surrounding him.

The voice who called Abram is the same voice who called Elijah, Isaiah, Peter, Matthew, Cromwell, Luther, myself, and shall call you! God simply repeats His call to those whom He calls, saying the same thing to each one of us:

> "Come out from among them and be separate," says the Lord. (2 Cor. 6:17a)

Let me say this again: *The call of God always demands separation*, a clear separation from anything that could steal the glory of God!

2. We Must Be Ready to Let Go

> Now the LORD said to Abram, "Go forth from your country, and from your relatives and from your father's house." (Gen. 12:1a NASB)

Abram was comfortable in his land and had more than sufficient supplies to meet his needs. He was deeply rooted in the commerce of the area and was passively residing in the security of family and friends, living comfortably in his father's house. Abram was what we consider to be advanced in age, some seventy-five years old. He was not exactly looking for big change, for sure.

This is the way God works. The call of God will demand that we leave the grip of all that makes us self-sufficient and secure in this world. Truth is, any real advancement of your divine call and purpose will involve both an altar on which some piece of the past life must be offered, sacrificed, and abandoned, and it will demand that you walk away from the cherished idols and relationships you once worshiped, enjoyed, and thought was for your good. Yes, even old friendships now will be unacceptable for your calling. You must be ready to let go of all that God commands you to in order to fulfill your calling!

This letting-go process is what separation accomplishes; it strips us of our self-made security, relationships and encumbrances then forces us to look to our Lord God as our everything!

In fact, this letting go is a major theme in Abram's life. He was to let go of his fatherland, family, and even his nephew, Lot. He was to become a sojourner in a land that was not his own as a pilgrim and stranger. God called him to let go of his own methods of fulfilling the process called life. Why? All of this was to bring Abram into a true fellowship and follow-ship with the one, true God!

I will take nothing, from a thread to a sandal strap, and that I will not take anything that is yours, lest you should say, "I have made Abram rich." (Gen. 14:23)

The goal of letting go is clear. God desires us to have an intimate fellowship with Him and a complete dependence on Him. We can never achieve this without letting go of the past, of any attachment that would prevent or encumber us from obeying the call of God.

The goal may be simple, but the implementation is anything but. Truth is, many cannot or will not endure such a test so severe and searching in its demands. They go away sorrowful from the One to whom they had come to with such zeal and hunger. This reminds me of the rich young ruler:

Then Jesus, looking at him, loved him, and said to him, "One thing you lack: Go your way, sell whatever you have and give to the poor, and you will have treasure in heaven; and come, take up the cross, and follow Me." But he was sad at this word, and went away sorrowful, for he had great possessions. (Mark 10:21–22)

3. We Must Be Willing to Go with Not-Knowing Obedience

To a land that I will show you. (Gen. 12:1b)

By faith Abraham obeyed when he was called to go out to the place which he would receive as an inheritance. And he went out, not knowing where he was going. (Heb. 11:8)

Abram was told to leave, but notice that he was told nothing of the land that God would give him. There was no slick video sales pitch of the premium, beachfront property the Lord had for him. There wasn't any picture portfolio showing how amazing this new land would be.

The Firebox: Demands of a Divine Call

God just called him out of where he was to something that would be defined at some other time! Therefore, his reaction here is the essence of not-knowing obedience!

Many times, God holds back the details in a divine call. He purposely leaves out specifics to place us in the position to fully trust Him as we obey. Here is the great challenge in obeying God's call in our lives. However, without this obedience to His call, nothing of the promise will take place. Without this obedience, you cannot become the voice of fire that you desire to be. Keep in mind that the promises to follow were conditional. They only took place if Abram exercised not-knowing obedience! It goes without saying that this places great importance on obedience for those who desire to become a voice of fire. In fact, the Bible clearly says:

> Has the Lord as great delight in burnt offerings and sacrifices, as in obeying the voice of the Lord? Behold, to obey is better than sacrifice, and to heed than the fat of rams. (1 Sam. 15:22)

4. We Must Have Faith That Follows

> So Abram departed as the Lord had spoken to him, and Lot went with him. And Abram was seventy-five years old when he departed from Haran. Then Abram took Sarai his wife and Lot his brother's son, and all their possessions that they had gathered, and the people whom they had acquired in Haran, and they departed to go to the land of Canaan. So they came to the land of Canaan. Abram passed through the land to the place of Shechem, as far as the terebinth tree of Moreh. And the Canaanites were then in the land. (Gen 12:4–6)

The Bible reveals that Abram went forth as the Lord had commanded and spoken. The evidence of Abram's faith was in his instant obedience to the word of the Lord! Now understand, this was not some kind of natural migration of families. Nor, did Abram say to himself, "I will put my house on the market, and if it sells, I will go!" None of this happened. Abram just gathered his things and went even though he could have expressed many excuses. He could have said, "Let me think about this a while and decide later," or "I'm too old for this kind of change in my life," or "My wife and I are too old to make a journey like this." But he didn't make any excuse at all, not even one question, no complaining, not a single word, only faith that followed the call of God! If we are to become a voice of fire, we must have faith that is willing to follow the call of God without a single question, word, or excuse.

I want you to notice this, "And the Canaanites were then in the land." Throughout the book of Genesis, the Canaanites were the antagonists who constantly caused problems and concerns at every turn. So, God was calling Abram to the Promised Land inhabited by Canaanites who were pagans—the enemy. This would mean that possessing this land as rightful heirs would not be without difficulty and trials, even war.

So, as a voice of fire, here is a caution as you engage in God's call: *Each time you obey, expect to encounter opposition.*

Too many times, we can be drawn into the belief that if we just obey God and His call on our lives, everything will be lovely. Well, this is just not true. Each and every time we obey God we are moving against the forces of this world and the rulers of evil. As a voice of fire, we must expect that there will be opposition and difficulty as we faithfully follow God.

There was a time when, as a church, we were in the planning stage of a new building. God had led us to our land, we had purchased it, and now He had blessed us with a donation of $200,000 to build our church! It was such an amazing time. All sorts of emotions were racing inside of me: tons of excitement, anticipation, longing to see it completed, and wondering what God would have for us as we moved forward. But I had some distance relatives of the Canaanites who would push back on everything we were trying to accomplish. They greatly opposed the building process, telling me that God had told them I was wrong, and I should not build a building. It made some days very difficult to push forward and caused me to petition the Lord many times to ask Him for relief. Anyway, my point is just that as we obey, we expect to run into opposition. It will come. Be strong and courageous and *press in, press on, and press through*!

Please, speak this truth out loud as though it is real: "*I am called of God!*"

The great news with obedience is the promises that follow.

The Great Promise of a Divine Call

> I will make you a great nation; I will bless you and make your name great; And you shall be a blessing. I will bless those who bless you, and I will curse him who curses you; and in you all the families of the earth shall be blessed. (Gen. 12:2–3)

God tells Abram, "*I will!*" These words refer to a covenant, a promise that God would be all he ever needed! So many times, God's commands are *not* accompanied by His reasons for giving them, but they are always accompanied by His promise, expressed or understood. Why is this? It is simple; we can understand a promise but probably would not understand God's reason. We believe God's reason would baffle and confuse us more than it would help us. Can you imagine the finite understanding the infinite? This is what His reason would be, a divine, infinite reason we could never fully understand. But a promise is something we can get; it is practical, positive, and literal! I love this. If Abram obeyed the call of God, he would be the vessel God would use to open up the blessings of the Lord to the families of all the earth. Wow!

When We Obey God's Commands, We Open the Unlimited Nature of God's Promises

This truth is powerful to such a degree that even the world can be touched and blessed by our blessings from the Almighty. Oh, if we could grasp this truth as voices of fire that as we obey the call of God to become a voice of fire, we place ourselves in position to be used of God, blessed by Him, and to impact all people we meet throughout this world. This is staggering. It just takes your breath! You can be that person!

The call of God creates the firebox for the voice of fire to reside in, the place that it can erupt, be stoked, and burn freely! It is in coming to this place in your life that you know you are called of God and are willing to submit your will to His will. This is where the voice of fire can burn the brightest and have the most impact! Are you willing to say yes to the call of God? If so, I declare over you: *You will become a voice of fire!*

5

The Firebrick: Risky Obedience

THE FIREBRICKS ARE DESIGNED TO be the place where the fire rests as it burns. Whether it is intense heat, medium flames, or only small embers, the firebricks receive the risky fire and contain it, making sure the heat is guided into the direction it was designed.

To surrender your life and become a voice of fire is a very risky step as we see it.

In fact, let's be clear: *Faithfully following Christ is risky.*

To abandon all and follow Christ continually places us outside of our comfort zones. Why? Each and every Christian has that place of obedience God has commanded right now in their walk that is risky to them if they go there. To some, it may be:

- Testimony: Getting up in front of people to give a testimony—risky obedience required. The devil will tell say can't do it, you will make a fool of yourself, you will stumble over your words, you just won't make sense, people will laugh at you, or you can't because you are very nervous.

- Evangelism: Walking up and down the street, knocking on doors to talk with people about Christ and the church—risky obedience required. Will they slam the door in your face?
- Prayer: Praying out loud in a group of people—risky obedience required. What will they think of me?
- Ministry: Traveling downtown to feed the homeless, sharing the Word of God and ministering to their needs—risky obedience required. The idea of beginning a ministry in a church—can it have impact?

I could go on and on. To genuinely follow Christ continually, calls me to step outside of "me" and place my full dependence on Christ. This is a good thing. God is calling us to be Christians who are willing to follow Christ with risky obedience.

I would like to give you a great example of faithful, risky obedience to Christ. It involves Paul's (named Saul at the time) conversion experience. Many times, we find ourselves only focusing on Paul and everything that happened to him.

> Then Saul arose from the ground, and when his eyes were opened he saw no one. But they led him by the hand and brought him into Damascus. And he was three days without sight, and neither ate nor drank. (Acts 9:8–9)

I would like to place our focus on another faithful character in this story. During Paul's conversion, there was a faithful man named Ananias who was a believer living in Damascus.

> Now there was a certain disciple at Damascus named Ananias. (Acts 9:10)

The Firebrick: Risky Obedience

This is really the only time that we hear of Ananias except when Paul shares the story of his conversion. What we know is that Ananias' ministry is a very brief work and consisted only of the one, short meeting with Paul. So, Ananias comes into the biblical spotlight for just a moment as God required something from him. Even though it was short-lived, Ananias did with great excellence what he was called to do by the Lord. Ananias had to exercise risky obedience to accomplish his assigned task for the Lord.

Fact is, we all don't always have major roles and offices in Christian service! God decides what part we are to play in His purpose.

Whatever Part We Have, We Are to Be Faithful and Do Our Best

We are to perform the part that God gives us to the best of our ability knowing that this is His will; whether God gives us a major or a minor part should not be our focus of importance. God will not consider major or minor because it all is major to Him; He looks at how faithful we are in doing what He has commanded.

> And whatever you do, do it heartily, as to the Lord and not to men, knowing that from the Lord you will receive the reward of the inheritance. (Col. 3:23–24)

> Moreover, it is required in stewards that one be found faithful. (1 Cor. 4:2)

> His lord said to him, "Well done, good and faithful servant; you were faithful over a few things, I will make you ruler over many things. Enter into the joy of your lord." (Matt. 25:21)

God demands us to be faithful servants over the few, the small, and the minor, and our great reward shall follow. Ananias clearly does his work faithfully as to the Lord, even though it was very risky! Ananias' call from God demanded risky obedience, and he obeyed God completely. This will be a great example for us as his firebrick produced a focused fire that changed the world for Christ! It is very important that we become a faithful, obedient risk taker for Christ, following hard after Him. Yes!

I want us to look at this more completely. I will identify the attributes of a faithful servant who is willing to engage God's will with risky obedience, laying the firebrick as a voice of fire. I call this:

The Four Attributes of a Faithful Risk Taker

1. We Must Be People of High Character

    There is no substitute for high character with God.

    A. A High Character Person Is Devoted to Christ

    Now there was a certain disciple at Damascus named Ananias. (Acts 9:10a)

Being a disciple in Damascus when Saul (Paul) was coming to persecute Christians speaks of Ananias' pure devotion to Christ. Ananias was no Sunday morning Christian. He was not found lacking in dedication, loyalty, faithfulness, willingness, and trust. He was a man devoted to Christ who would stand firm in the darkest of times, and this was a very dark time for real Christians. Saul, himself, was on the way to throw Christians in jail at the very least and perhaps even kill them out right! Ananias was living in very evil and dark times when it was extremely difficult to trust other people you did not know. However, Ananias was a disciple of Christ in spite of the risk.

This is where a voice of fire starts: completely devoted to Christ. Being named by others as a disciple of Christ says it all. In other words, our actions and words must be aligned with the Lord Jesus Christ. When others see us, they say, "There goes a disciple of Christ." When others don't see us, God says, "There goes my disciple."

B. A High Character Person Is Devoted to God's Word

> And a certain Ananias, a man who was devout by the standard of the Law. (Acts 22:12 NASB)

I am not talking about a legalist or Pharisee who would strain at a gnat but swallow a camel. Nor am I talking about a person who majored on the minor things while minoring on the major things. The verse is saying that Ananias lived his life measured by the holy law of God.

Oh, that today believers would be careful to align their lives and devotion measured by the Word of God. Too much today we seem to depend on our friends, self-help books, famous personalities, or accolades from others to shape our devotion. This idea that devotion to Jesus Christ is controlled by what others think and the popular persuasion of the day is just wrong! God's Word clearly teaches us that anything less than giving Christ *all* is falling short of His desire for us. As a voice of fire, complete devotion to God's Word is the only acceptable position on which we must settle.

C. A Person of High Character Lives a Consistently Godly Life

> And well spoken of by all the Jews who lived there. (Acts 22:12b ESV)

Ananias lived a faithful life before his own people, and it was noticed. They could not find fault or condemn him. This clearly says that our godly conduct should be a good advertisement for the church and for Christ as we live our lives to reach others in our community and around the world. A voice of fire will live righteously before the world as an example of how Christ impacts a life, and God will use us to draw people to Him!

2. We Must Be People Attuned to the Voice of God

> And the Lord said to him in a vision, "Ananias." And he said, "Behold, here am I, Lord." And the Lord said to him, "Get up and go to the street called Straight, and inquire at the house of Judas for a man from Tarsus named Saul, for behold, he is praying, and he has seen in a vision a man named Ananias come in and lay his hands on him, so that he might regain his sight." (Acts 9:10–12 NASB)

A. A Person Ready to Serve

"Behold, here am I." (Acts 9:10 NASB)

This is the language of a person listening for the voice of God. Ananias was standing in the ready and waiting position to hear from the Lord and was prepared to receive His instructions.

So many believers today miss out on doing God's will simply because they are not in the listening position or standing ready to say, "Behold, here am I." They are just not in the ready mode for service for the Lord. The reasons for this are the many distractions of this world that cause so much noise that they miss the clear voice of Christ calling their names.

Truth is: *Our primary responsibility in life is to do God's will.*

> Jesus said to them, "My food is to do the will of Him who sent Me, and to accomplish His work." (John 4:34 ESV)

It is never a lack of opportunity that will keep us from serving our Lord, but rather, it is a lack of readiness. Becoming a voice of fire will require your full attention and concentration on being ready for both

The Firebrick: Risky Obedience

hearing your name called and being ready for service. We must let God take care of opportunity; whatever comes from our Lord, our only response must be, "Behold, here am I!"

B. A Person Ready to Receive Instruction

Ananias was ready to hear from God. When he heard his name called, he answered quickly with, "I'm here, ready to listen to God's heart." When God calls our name, He always has something for us to learn and do!

I want you to see the breakdown of God's clear and direct communication to Ananias.

First, God told him where to go. "Arise and go to the street called Straight." This is exactly how God operates. He gets our attention by calling our name, and then He proceeds to give us instruction. Ananias was told exactly where to go: the street called Straight. We may have not yet received a grand vision from the Lord for our lives, we may lack knowledge or even be lacking in wisdom, but God clearly tells us what is important when giving us a task to do. Our place of service will be made clear.

Second, He was told whom to find. "And inquire at the house of Judas for one called Saul of Tarsus, for behold, he is praying." OK, wait a minute. Ananias was told to go and find Saul of Tarsus! This is the same Saul who was coming to create havoc, arrest Christians, and perhaps even get them killed. But it is clear that Ananias was strong and courageous! In fact, he was a man of great courage to obey God's call to go and find Saul the persecutor of Christians!

For sure, we can learn: *It will take courage to serve the Lord without question.*

Third, Ananias was told what to do! "And in a vision, he has seen a man named Ananias coming in and putting his hand on him, so that he might receive his sight." God was calling Ananias to go to the one who was persecuting the believers in Christ and bring healing to his blind eyes; God was calling Ananias to do the impossible. Some would say, "I can't do this!" and just not go. But we must always remember, God is in the business of the impossible.

This, without question, teaches us: *God never calls us to do something we cannot do.*

Hear this: even if we do not yet see an ability that may be required to accomplish what God is commanding us to do manifested in our Christian walk, God will provide it during our obedience. Or let me say it like this: Many times, the needed ability shall be manifested "as we are going," and what is needed shall be given!

For an example: You might say, "I don't have the gift of healing, so I will not go." You may have just missed out on seeing God's great gifting manifested though you! Many times, God gives us what we need in ministry as we are being obedient, going and ministering just as He has said. Unless you go, you miss out on His great, divine will and gifting for you and the deliverance and healing of others!

Voices of fire are always ready to hear their names called by God, standing ready to receive His instructions.

3. We Must Be Real Before the Lord

> But Ananias answered, "Lord, I have heard from many about this man, how much harm he did to Your saints at Jerusalem; and here he has authority from the chief priests to bind all who call upon Your name. (Acts 9:13–14 NASB)

Right here, the temptation is to push back on this command, maybe asking God, "Are you sure about this?" or "God, do you know who this guy is?" This is definitely what the flesh would say, and even the enemy would seed this in your mind.

But this is not what was recorded in the Word of God. In fact, Ananias was only stating the facts as he understood them. First, he was being real by taking his concerns to the Lord directly. I am sure this command didn't come to Ananias without concerns. But he was not telling God he wouldn't do it; he was just being real with God after hearing what He was commanding him to do. God is never upset at us for sharing our concerns!

> Casting all your anxiety upon Him, because He [God] cares for you. (1 Peter 5:7)

Second, he was being real by seeking assurance with a willingness to serve. This is key. Our hearts should always be in the willingness to serve position. It was not wrong for him to seek God's assurance when the calling was a dangerous or unusual assignment. The only requirement is a willingness to do the task as asked by the Lord.

As voices of fire, being real in our conversations with the Lord about our concerns is a great place to air them out. This is the right place to get it straightened out with clear understanding. How can we be impactful in the call unless we are operating with a heart full of confidence that this is exactly what God desires? Anything less than full confidence will breed doubt, hesitation, and reduce our ministry impact.

4. We Must Be Willing to Instantly Obey

> And Ananias went his way and entered the house; and laying his hands on him he said, "Brother Saul, the Lord Jesus, who appeared to you on the road as you came, has sent me that you may receive your sight and be filled with the Holy Spirit." Immediately there fell from his eyes something like scales, and he received his sight at once; and he arose and was baptized. So when he had received food, he was strengthened. (Acts 9:17–19)

So, after Ananias' conversation with the Lord and he was given God's intent and his heart was enlightened, Ananias immediately obeyed God's call and went to find Saul. In all human terms, this was stupid and downright nuts! This is exactly what the flesh and the enemy would say, "Don't go, don't do it, don't be stupid."

Understand: *The purpose of enlightenment is obedience.*

Get this: God tells him to go, and Ananias immediately departed, located Saul (Paul), and entered into the persecutor's house. This is very risky obedience! But understand, God will send you where there are problems to be solved. Our risky obedience will always have God's purpose behind it.

God's purpose in sending Ananias was for Saul to receive his sight, "Immediately there fell from his eyes something like scales, and he received his sight at once," to be filled with the Holy Spirit and for his baptism. Here we have all three of these accomplished. Why? A man, called by God, ready to hear and full of risky obedience, results in a man being set free and empowered to take the gospel to the world in power! Truly, because of Ananias' amazing obedience to God, you and I are believers today.

Voices of fire must always be ready, willing, and determined to accomplish God's instructions to the fullest. No matter the cost, no matter what gifting you may have now, no matter how risky it seems, voices of fire are called to be Christians who are willing to follow Christ with risky obedience even if it appears to require your life! If you are, I declare over you: *You will become a voice of fire!*

While I was on one of my many Philippines mission trips in the southernmost island of Mindanao, risky obedience became very real to me. Just to get to Diplog, Mindanao takes two to three days of traveling—not what you would call a stroll in the park. You travel from the US to Tokyo, Japan, have a long layover and then go from Tokyo to Manila, Philippines—twenty-five to thirty hours of travel. You now find

The Firebrick: Risky Obedience

yourself with a thirteen-hour time difference and your nights are now days and your days are now nights! Your body struggles to cooperate with the time-change demands. You spend the night, if you can sleep, and rise early to take the first flight out, heading to Diplog, Mindanao.

Diplog was our home-base of ministry while in the Philippines. This particular time, our ministry in the Philippines took us southwest of Diplog, about a four-hour drive to a town named Ipil. The partnering ministry had scheduled a three-night crusade in Ipil, Mindanao. This crusade would be held at a public center; it would host around five thousand people.

We drove four hours that day, arrived in Ipil, and all was fine. We did make one peculiar stop. During our journey, we stopped by an army post with our ministry lead saying that he wanted to say hello to a friend. The friend was found, and they had a good visit, not that I understood a word they were saying because they were speaking in their native tongue, the Tagalog language. It was no more than a thirty-minute stop, so we continued to the lodging we would use for the next three to four days of ministry.

That night, around 6:30 pm, they came to pick me up to travel over to the public center so we could host our first crusade of this mission trip. I was excited and a little on edge for two reasons. First, Ipil had been attacked in the past by some two hundred heavily armed Abu Sayyaf militants (a Jihadist terror group based in this area of the Philippines) who randomly fired upon people in the streets, ransacked homes, plundered banks, took hostages, and burned the center of the town to the ground! Over a hundred people were killed, and hundreds were wounded. This group, the Abu Sayyaf militants, was considered to be very violent and responsible for bombings, kidnappings, assassinations, rape, child sexual assault, drive-by shootings, drug trafficking, and extortion as they demanded their own land within the Philippines. So, Ipil had been a victim of violence in the past.

Second, this same group had kidnapped Martin and Gracia Burnham, missionaries to the Philippines, holding them for ransom. This group was known for cutting off your head if the money was not paid! In fact, our driver was to be our security, and he was carrying a gun for our protection. So, evil was all around.

Now, as we pulled up to the public center, I saw many people entering the center and activity all around the place. This was exciting to see such opportunity to preach to so many people. I still couldn't tell how many, but my mind was racing with excitement to preach the Word of God!

My thoughts were interrupted by our driver saying, "Please, stay in the car." I was puzzled by this. I'm there to preach the gospel, to reach people for Christ, and to see the power of God rain down on us! I am ready, but they say stay and wait. Due to the language barrier, I was frustrated as to why we were waiting.

Then when looking out of my window, I saw a soldier holding a dog on a leash. This was not a common thing for me to see in the US. I was thinking, "I wonder what is going on?" The soldier approached our vehicle and spoke with our driver. Again, I didn't understand anything they were saying, but I really wished I could at that moment.

After they finished their discussion, the driver turned to me and said, "OK, you can get out now." Well, I had to ask why we needed to wait and what the soldier doing here. The driver responded, "The soldier told me that he had walked the whole center with his bomb-sniffing dog, and that they didn't find any bombs! He felt like it was safe for me to go inside."

I was stunned when he told me this information. I hadn't thought about it, it hadn't entered my mind, I hadn't planned for it, nor had we had any discussions about this kind of concern with the ministry team. Wow, we needed a bomb-sniffing dog to move through the center just before I went inside! I had to take a moment, pause, and say a prayer! "Lord, you called me here, and I am trusting you for my protection by faith! So, I go in risky obedience to accomplish what you have called me to do." I opened the door and walked inside full of confidence in my God and His purpose for these people. We had about forty-five hundred people come to hear the gospel and more than five hundred people received Christ as their Savior and Lord! Following the service, hundreds were healed by the power of God. God truly blesses risky obedience that will be required as we serve Him!

The real question is: Will you become a faithful risk taker for the Lord? Not foolish, but faithful!

If you are to become a voice of fire, you must answer yes to this question. God will purposefully place you in situations and spiritual challenges that will require risky obedience. This doesn't need to be half way around the world. It can and will be required right where you are, serving where you are right now! It can be required as you go and tell others about Christ. It can be required as you feed the hungry or pray for the sick. It can be required as you are used in the body of Christ. This is something that you must prepare yourself for and be ready to exercise risky obedience! If so, I declare over you: *You will become a voice of fire!*

6

The Fire Starter: Great Faith

FIRE STARTERS ARE ESPECIALLY SELECTED small pieces of tinder or wood that are very dry and ready for a spark to begin the fire. By design, this material is so dry and combustible that with a tiny spark, it will burst into flames, creating the genesis for a continuing blaze.

I've had the great privilege to travel all over the world taking the gospel to many nations. Every nation, every country, every city, every community, and every tribe is ready, primed, and waiting for spiritual fire starters—men and women burning with a spiritual flame, committed to His Word, full of faith, believing for things that do not exist as though they do exist, and not worried about their reputation but faithful to His Word no matter the cost personally. They are willing and ready to place their faith on the line, asking and believing God to even raise the dead. What more can I say? This is one of the greatest needs we face today.

I believe church leadership in the United States has moved away from this fire-starter person of God to a mindset of success-driven leadership as defined by church size, money in the bank, reaching mega church status, and seekers at all cost, rather than embracing the fire starters of our generation. I see the church as reaching a very dangerous tipping point. Many times, the church shuns and even considers fire starters as outcasts, people to avoid.

Just last week, I had a conversation with a man who considers himself a godly man and a good leader within the church. As we engaged in conversation, he began to make statements without appropriate biblical understanding. In fact, I think he was lecturing me on what a successful church must look like based only on what he had been taught or believed, not solely on God's Word! I tried to engage him with an overall scriptural position, but he would only revert to coined phrases he had learned. He just wouldn't listen to a full, biblical explanation. This is a major problem. I repeat, we are in desperate need of spiritual fire starters today! So, as a voice of fire, I, too, will be a fire starter!

God, we call upon You to raise up fire starters all over the world and allow them to be heard. Let them be the tinder as you, oh God, provide the spark so that they erupt into a flame, creating the beginning of a blaze that others will keep on burning!

This leads us to the question: What is the single greatest need for a person to be a voice of fire and a fire starter? What really matters as a voice of fire operating within the context of bringing fire to others? It is clear to me that voices of fire must be people of great faith who are willing to exercise it wherever they go. I would like us to look at this through the eyes of a man who demonstrated great faith, believing the impossible shall happen—a man named Elijah.

I want to be very clear: Elijah was a man of great faith, but he was only a man. James clearly points this out for our instruction.

> Elijah was a man with a nature like ours, and he prayed earnestly that it would not rain; and it did not rain on the land for three years and six months. And he prayed again, and the heaven gave rain, and the earth produced its fruit. (James 5:17–18 ESV)

The word *nature* here means similarly affected. Elijah was similarly affected just like anyone: just like me, just like you. He was human, yet, he prayed earnestly that it wouldn't rain, and it did not rain! For three years and six months, the heavens were closed because he asked, believing God. Then after three years and six months, Elijah prayed again, believing God, and He opened the heavens, and it poured rain! If Elijah, who had a nature like ours and could be used by God in this way, so can we! I say again, Elijah was a man of great faith.

Which leads us to: *Elijah was God's instrument who had great faith to believe the impossible.*

Many times, as we move by faith, we are confronted with the impossible; we just can't see a way forward. There even doesn't seem to be a way around it or through it. At that moment, it's time to take it to God Almighty, and the impossible now becomes the possible!

In fact: *God specializes in impossible situations.*

God does what we cannot do. The Scriptures reveal this for us to see plainly.

> Ah, Lord God! Behold, You have made the heavens and the earth by Your great power and outstretched arm. There is nothing too hard for You. (Jer. 32:17)

> But He said, "The things which are impossible with men are possible with God." (Luke 18:27)

God Uses Devastating Circumstances to Usher in the Need for Great Faith

Elijah was faced several times with situations in his life we would call devastating. However, the one I would like us to look at is when Elijah had to travel to Zarephath and meet the very poor widow who was in great need. God had instructed Elijah to go, and He would persuade a widow to provide for him. The problem was that she had nothing left. In fact, she only had enough provision to make one more batch of bread, and then she and her son would eat it and wait to die. When Elijah arrived, he intervened and instructed her on what to do and promised there would be no end to the ingredients needed for bread. And the miracle began with provision for each day by God Almighty! So, Elijah settled into life with the widow and her son. He was comfortably enjoying God's provision and was under God's protection from King Ahab who wanted to find him and kill him. Suddenly, the peaceful, comfortable day-in and day-out routine was shattered with a devastating circumstance which ushered in a need for great faith! Such a devastating circumstance requiring a miracle had never been recorded in the Scripture.

> Now it happened after these things that the son of the woman who owned the house became sick. And his sickness was so serious that there was no breath left in him. So she said to Elijah, "What have I to do with you, O man of God? Have you come to me to bring my sin to remembrance, and to kill my son?" (1 Kings 17:17–18)

The widow's only son, her only loved one on this earth, died! The word *breath* here is the same word used when God created Adam and breathed into his nostrils the breath of life. So, "no breath" clearly meant her son was dead! All her future plans and dreams lay dead in her arms, gone forever! It is clear she felt hopeless, condemned, and even judged for her sins. Her heart was full of sorrow, grief, and sadness. She was totally overwhelmed with grief by this devastating reality. She did what many do when devastating circumstances arrive on their doorstep. She struck out and blamed Elijah and God for her troubles!

Elijah, the man of God, was moved with compassion and saw past her grief and anger. I love this about Elijah. He cared about the people he was with, so much so that he didn't take even a moment to defend himself or his God! He didn't argue with her on what she said. He grieved with her and helped to bear the weight of her pain compassionately and in silence. Then, he just moved past all this emotion and grief and chose to take action! Elijah said, "Give me your son." Why would he want her dead son? What was he going to do? Go bury him? I believe these four words are among the greatest examples of faith in all the Bible: "Give me your son." Elijah didn't know what God would do in this devastating reality. He had no guarantees for her, only His great faith in his God! Why would he do this? Because Elijah knew the God of impossibilities, and he would take the dead boy to his God! Elijah's request was immediately embraced by the widow as his statement perhaps brought a ray of hope and light in a very dark moment within her heart. She instantly gave her son with no hesitation.

Let's look together at:

Four Actions of Great Faith

Real faith demands action. Understand: Faith without action is only a dream. In fact, action without faith is just filling time. But, faith with action can change any circumstance! So, let's look together at the four actions that support great faith.

1. Great Faith Demands Alone-Time with God Prior to a Need

   So he took him out of her arms and carried him to the upper room where he was staying, and laid him on his own bed. Then he cried out to the Lord and said, "O Lord my God, have You also brought tragedy on the widow with whom I lodge, by killing her son?" (1 Kings 17:19–20)

After taking the widow's son, Elijah retreats to his private place of prayer where he would pour his heart out to God and call on His mercy! This is his everyday place of meeting God alone, a place he has met God in the past where God has revealed His presence, direction, provision, and promises. It also was a place where doubt was dispelled, fear was cast out, and trust swelled to the heights of great mountains. It was where great faith was shaped, nourished, and embraced. Elijah was just taking this major, difficult, impossible problem to the God he believed in!

> He who dwells in the secret place of the Most High shall abide under the shadow of the Almighty. I will say of the Lord, "He is my refuge and my fortress; my God, in Him I will trust." Surely He shall deliver you from the snare of the fowler and from the perilous pestilence. He shall cover you with His feathers, and under His wings you shall take refuge; His truth shall be your shield and buckler. (Ps. 91:1–4)

This is something we all must have: an alone place where we meet God. A place we have met Him in the past. A place where we can talk to the Lord about doubt, fear, direction, trust, and obedience. A place where we sense His peace and presence. A place where panic flees. A place where fear will be displaced with faith and doubt is not allowed. A place we can go and meet God while in crises because we have met Him there in everyday life. It's our place to do regular business together with Him. It is a familiar place of meeting God, one-on-one. This is where we prepare ourselves for life. Without this meeting place, we lack the necessary rock in the foundation of our faith that will be shaped into great faith over time! This is where Elijah took the dead son—to the place where he met his God every day.

2. Great Faith Demands Undiminished Faith

> And he stretched himself out on the child three times, and cried out to the Lord and said, "O Lord my God, I pray, let this child's soul come back to him." (1 Kings 17:21)

The Fire Starter: Great Faith

In this private place where he met God every day, Elijah petitioned Him for the son's life. He prayed a simple but great prayer of faith: "Let this child's life return to him." Not one time, or two times, but three times he stretched himself out on the son, asking God for the impossible miracle of life for the dead boy, body-to-body, arm-to-arm, leg-to-leg, completely covering this boy with his faith. At this moment, God viewed this boy through Elijah's great faith. Have you ever wondered how long it was between each prayer? A minute or minutes or an hour—we do not know. However, we are now dealing with the impossible that God makes possible. The natural, physiological rules were thrown out. Christ was in the grave three days and then came back to life; nothing is impossible with God!

Wow! What a moment this must have been. Elijah stretched over the dead son, asking with great faith for God to do the impossible and return life to him! I wonder where the voices of fire are who would do something like this today. Who would have such great faith to believe their God, so much so as to stretch over the dead, asking with great faith for God do the impossible and return life to them?

I would love to share a story that occurred while I was just moving through my normal day. I received a call from a nurse who attended my church. She proceeded to share with me that a twenty-one-year-old student from India was in her hospital's ICU. He had come down with a very high fever and was now on life support. His organs were shutting down. The doctors were not very encouraging about his prognosis. His mother and father were called in India, and they were arranging a flight to come to the United States. I could hear Christ like compassion in her voice. She requested that we place the boy on our prayer list and pray fervently that God would heal him. Of course we will, I shared with her.

The next Sunday morning, the nurse came into service with the young boy's parents. Of course, they were very distressed. They were not believers in Christ; in fact, they were followers of Hinduism. At the end of our service, she brought the parents down for prayer. As I prayed for the son, the Lord put in my spirit to declare this young son to "come forth" in the name of Jesus! I had never used this call before in the prayer of healing. I was surprised but standing in God's power to heal.

The next few days did not return any good news at all. The reports each day from our nurse reached a point where the boy was placed on life support with no visible signs of life! For all practical purposes, the doctors were just waiting on the parents to agree to take him off life support and allow the boy to die. The parents were overwhelmed with grief. God would not let me rest.

On the following Wednesday night after Sunday's service, I traveled to the hospital with a companion. As I arrived at the ICU and started to enter the room, a nurse asked me a few questions and then instructed me to put on protective gown, gloves, and mask due to the fact that they didn't know what had caused his condition. So, I dressed as required by the nurse and then entered the room.

Upon entry, my spiritual senses were overwhelmed. Death hung in the room like tree moss in the Everglades. It was so thick it felt as though I could cut it with a knife. Oppressive, dark, demonic activity was all around. Chills shivered down my spine. It was almost like I could hear the chant, "He is ours, he is ours!" crying out all around me. Now, let's be clear, this was a very uncomfortable and restless place to be—certainly not a place for the timid of spiritual heart. However, I was there by the His hand. Therefore, I would call upon the God of impossibilities to do what the doctors were saying was not possible.

I approached him as he lay in the bed with tubes in his mouth and arms and with machines forcing his lungs to breathe and heart to beat. His eyes were mostly closed. My mind and heart raced. God placed in my spirit this very story of Elijah and the widow's son who had died. So, following the example of Elijah's great faith, I stretched over this young boy and began to pray that God would breathe life back into

The Fire Starter: Great Faith

him! I stretched out and prayed once, twice, and, yes, even a third time, asking for a great miracle from our God. Each time I prayed, I paused for three to five minutes to wait upon the Lord's response.

Something significant happened after the third time. The young boy's eyelids opened, and I could look into his eyes. They were black and cold looking, but I didn't see that as anything other than God telling me He was at work! This encouraged my faith to believe God was working. I then left the room under no fanfare from the doctors or nurses or even the hospital staff. To them it was a non-event. I arrived and left with little notice or concern. But, I believed that God was moving heaven and earth to accomplish a miracle at that very moment! The next morning, I received a phone message from the nurse. She was almost breathless. She reported that it was a miracle; the boy's organs were beginning to function again, and there was hope! The next day, another call came from her with the report that his body functions were working perfectly, and the doctors were amazed. Then the following day, she reported they were taking him off life support, and that he was going to be fine! My heart leapt with great joy and total amazement in our loving God. Sometime later, the boy came to our church and accepted Christ as his Lord and Savior!

Our God has not changed. He is the same yesterday, today, and forever! The issue is, where are the voices of fire, like Elijah, who will even pray to bring back life from the dead? Does the thought ever cross your mind to pray that God will bring those who are dead back to life?

Elijah demonstrated undiminished faith as he prayed again and again, asking God to answer his prayer. A simple request, impossible for man, yet more than possible for God. Elijah didn't give up asking until he received the answer. This is undiminished faith. In fact, this kind of un-diminishing, persistent prayer is encouraged by the Lord.

> I say to you, though he will not rise and give to him because he is his friend, yet because of his persistence he will rise and give him as many

as he needs. So I say to you, ask, and it will be given to you; seek, and you will find; knock, and it will be opened to you. For everyone who asks receives, and he who seeks finds, and to him who knocks it will be opened. (Luke 11:8–10)

Voices of fire must become hearts with undiminished faith, willing and ready to pray persistently until the answer from God comes. Today we live in a microwave age of prayer. A few prayers, and that's it. No, I say! Stretch over the impossibility, ask again and again, apply your great faith, and wait patiently for God's answer.

3. Great Faith Believes God Can Do the Impossible

Then the Lord heard the voice of Elijah; and the soul of the child came back to him, and he revived. (1 Kings 17:22)

Elijah was asking for something totally unheard of. It had never been asked for in Scripture. It had never been performed. Therefore, to man it was totally impossible. So, for sure, Elijah was reaching for the impossible. You only reach for the impossible when great faith exists. See this playing out in your mind's eye: Elijah stretched out over the dead son once, twice, and the third time asking for the mercy of God to return life to him. Then, all of a sudden, as they are body-to-body, the son began to breathe, his fingers twitched, his arms began to shift, his legs moved, his eyes opened, and he stared into the eyes of Elijah, a man of great faith. So, this son saw what great faith actually looked like in real time! I think this would be a look never forgotten: the unforgettable eyes of great faith!

Truth is, Elijah saw, firsthand, that you can take the impossible, the never-been-done situation, to God, and it can become possible. If we are going be people of great faith, we start by taking the devastating situations of life to God with great faith that He will change things.

We know that the God of Elijah is your God, and He is still the God of impossibilities. Understand this: God desires to use you and your great faith in changing the impossible! Voices of fire expect and desire to be used of God to see the impossible become possible!

4. Great Faith Demonstrates Who God Is to Others

> And Elijah took the child and brought him down from the upper room into the house, and gave him to his mother. And Elijah said, "See, your son lives!" Then the woman said to Elijah, "Now by this I know that you are a man of God, and that the word of the Lord in your mouth is the truth." (1 Kings 17:23–24)

Now, Elijah got to be the bearer of great news to the mother. He brought him to her and told her the boy is alive! He didn't say, "Look what I have done" or "I told you so," he just said, "See, your son lives!" With this, Elijah was saying, "See, God is alive, all powerful, and full of mercy and kindness. My God is not like Baal; He is the one and true God!" Elijah really wanted her to see the real demonstration of who God was, not how great Elijah was. As God uses us, voices of fire will always point out to others how great our God is, not how great we are! When the woman saw her son alive, she did not see Elijah, but, rather, she saw the Lord! She then proclaimed that she knew that Elijah's God was the one, true God! Any result of our great faith must always lead people to believe God is real and point them to Christ our Lord! Nothing else will be executable.

The need for voices of fire is greater today than any time in history. There are people among us with devastating circumstances that seem impossible just like this widow. There are lives that are broken and bruised from the past where addictions have created a generation of dependence on everything other than God. People are lying dead and lifeless in their addictions, unable to feel, act, or have faith to cry out to God. They are paralyzed with inaction. People are living in violence, lust, greed, discontentment, selfishness, and pride. I could go on. This is where voices of fire can make a real difference. This is where great faith can be exercised with life-changing results.

There are corpses walking among us as well, people with real obstacles that seem to overwhelm them to a point that they can't move forward in the Lord. They have lost their passion for Christ, their faith is decreasing, and their love is fading; they have lost their desire for holiness. All of these things are sapping the spiritual strength from them. A voice of fire is needed with great faith to stretch out over them and ask Him to bring God-filled life back. We are to take their lifeless areas and ask God for the impossible: for life to return, for the impossible to become possible. God send the voices of fire among us!

God will never meet an intimidating obstacle He cannot overcome, never meet an enemy He cannot defeat, never see man's final decision He cannot override, nor will any powerful man ever be able to overshadow God. In fact, even death is not an obstacle God cannot overturn. God has infinite, unlimited power.

Voices of fire will believe in the God of impossibilities with great faith to reach the lost, heal the sick, raise the dead, and even more than we can imagine!

Do you have the faith to take these impossibilities before the Lord, before the God of impossibilities? If so, I declare over you: *You will become a voice of fire!*

7

The Fire Logs: A Ready Fire Needs Fuel

OVER THE NEXT SEVERAL CHAPTERS, I would like to address our part in this voice of fire. It has to do with placing good logs on to the fire to keep it going day after day, month after month, and even year after year! The fire logs are very important to the voice of fire. So many rely on the fire from past years, past months, or even last week. Understand that in order for the voice of fire to remain burning brightly and strong, logs must be added. This will be a considerable challenge in our lives to consistently supply the logs that will provide the fuel for the fire so that it will burn its hottest. It is one thing to start a fire start, but it is quite another to keep it burning with great intensity.

You will never be a voice of fire if you are afraid to stand for holy conduct, and holy conduct will demand a high price to be paid. For sure, the voice of compromise is very strong today, but we must be willing to pay this price and allow God to shape us into lives that demonstrate Christ is real and changes lives. Today is the time when truth must be heard!

In our home fireplaces, the type of wood used makes a huge difference in the temperature of the fire. We have found that the hottest fire burns with oak or logs of the hardwood family that are free of tree sap or moisture. So, each year we would look for a fallen oak tree that we could cut up and haul to our wood pile. So, the point is, the type of logs used makes a big difference in the quality of the fire.

We will now look at a few key spiritual logs that we must continue to place on our fire so that it continues to burn brightly. In order for us to remain voices of fire, there must be a fire inside of us burning with the will of God. So, let's take a look at the spiritual logs of holy conduct, preparation, prayer, and having the right perspective. Keep in mind, these are not the only logs for our fire, but certainly the following logs are of great importance to our voice of fire.

Price: Holy Conduct

FOR VOICES OF FIRE, HOLY conduct should be our heart's desire because we are called of God to holiness. God says:

> But as He who called you is holy, you also be holy in all your conduct. (1 Peter 1:15)

Holy conduct is purging sin from our daily walk, living righteously before others, and speaking in a godly way with all. Holy conduct must mirror God. God is love, and our holy conduct should reflect God's kind of love. In fact, the Bible teaches us that the fruit of the Holy Spirit is "love, joy, peace, longsuffering, kindness, goodness, faithfulness, gentleness, self-control. Against such there is no law" (Gal. 5:22–23). It continues to say that we have crucified the flesh with its passions and desires. If we live in the Spirit, let us also walk in the Spirit. This really is a great way of defining holy conduct. We should live our lives according to God and His Word. As we live in holy conduct, we can become like dry, seasoned hardwood for the fire that will burn best. And this kind of fire continues to produce the hottest voice of fire for the Lord.

Holy conduct doesn't even seem to be a target today. It is a task in which many are falling short of God's intent. Today, there is so much compromise, and it is done way too quickly on issues we face; we tell ourselves, "God didn't mean this situation." The Bible is very clear: we are called to Holy Spirit conduct. If we truly live this way, we will pay a high price. So, why is there such a high price for holy conduct?

Satan does not want others to see that Christ ushers in love, joy, peace, longsuffering, kindness, goodness, faithfulness, gentleness, and self-control into a person's life. So, each time he can get us to compromise on a life issue, he takes away a piece of our testimony of Christ.

I would like us to look at a man in the Bible who paid a very high price for holy conduct. His name was John the Baptist.

John the Baptist was man who appeared on the timeline of history six months before Christ pierced the darkness of this world. John was sent by God to prepare the way of the Lord. So, John was definitely called by God to do something for the preparation of Jesus Christ becoming the sin sacrifice for all people. Now, fast forward a few years, and we find John to be a voice of fire crying in the wilderness: "Make straight the way of the Lord." John was drawing large crowds of people coming to listen to him, and then they were being baptized. He was ministering six months before Christ came and began His ministry and journey to the cross. Sometime after Jesus came, John was arrested, and then he was beheaded. I don't know of very many people who would say yes to ministering for six months and then being killed; that's just not in your thought process when you desire to be used of God! This is what I call a high price for holy conduct.

The gruesome beheading of John the Baptist is one of the events that shows man at his very worst. It certainly underscores that the more a person is favored of God, the more the mistreatment of that person is likely by the world and by evil itself. Or another way of putting it is, the more a person demonstrates holy conduct, the more that person will be hated by the world.

Price: Holy Conduct

Let's take a closer look at this story in the Bible. I would like us to pick up the story of John the Baptist when he was in prison because of his preaching against Herod's sins.

> Herod the tetrarch, being rebuked by him concerning Herodias, his brother Philip's wife, and for all the evils which Herod had done, also added this, above all, that he shut John up in prison. (Luke 3:19)

Herod's sin was that he was in an adulterous marriage with his brother's wife as well as many other wicked things. History reveals to us that this adulterous marriage happened while he was on a trip to Rome. He stopped by to see his brother Philip and became infatuated with his wife, Herodias, and she with him. Herod takes her as his wife, revealing that this relationship was based upon nothing but the lust of the flesh, lust of the eyes, and the pride of life. This was the essence of raw, unadulterated, obvious sin in every way! John began preaching and openly rebuking Herod over his sinful ways.

> For Herod himself had sent and laid hold of John, and bound him in prison for the sake of Herodias, his brother Philip's wife; for he had married her. Because John had said to Herod, "It is not lawful for you to have your brother's wife." (Mark 6:17–18)

Truth is: *Standing for holy conduct will cost you.*

This is so true. If you take a stand for holy conduct, you will pay a price. This is exactly what a voice of fire will do. They will always take God's view on how people should live their lives. If we take a stand today and speak out against abortion, there will be an army of hate that will rise up against us. If we take a stand and speak out against divorce, a large percentage of people today will walk away, refusing to hear the Word of the Lord. If we take a stand today and speak out against the sinful homosexual lifestyle, we will be personally attacked, called all sorts of names, with the possibility of physical attacks from some who hate those who call out sin. If we take a stand today and speak out against drugs and alcohol in our city, many will despise you.

This is a truth that will challenge us: *Standing for biblical, holy conduct will produce enemies.*

Not that this should surprise us at all. Jesus said:

> Blessed are you when they revile and persecute you, and say all kinds of evil against you falsely for my sake. (Matt. 5:11)

This leads us to these powerful truths:

The High Price We Pay When We Stand for Holy Conduct

1. We Should Expect the World to Hate Us

> Therefore Herodias held it against him and wanted to kill him, but she could not. (Mark 6:19)

> And although he wanted to put him to death, he feared the multitude, because they counted him as a prophet. (Matt. 14:5)

Herod would not permit John to be killed only because of his own perception that the people might rise up against him. This was mostly because of political concerns; he was afraid of the people. They highly respected John and viewed him as a prophet from God. But let's be clear, both Herod and Herodias hated, loathed, and despised John with all their being. They simply could not tolerate his preaching against their sin and evil. Truth is that the indictment of sin will bring heated and hated reactions for those who are guilty.

As voices of fire living in holy conduct, there will be times we must speak the truth of God that will go against the ways of people. In fact, if you are not preaching truths that rub against people's lives today, you are not a voice of fire at all. God's truth is broad in nature and covers all aspects of our lives. You must preach the Word, and you will find His truth about people's behavior. In your preaching, you will reveal sinfulness. Not that you are selecting them out like we see here, but that you just share the Word of God, and thus some people in the world will hate you.

2. We Should Expect the World to Plot and Take Action against Us

> And a strategic [convenient] day came. (Mark 6:21 NASB)

This shows us that the execution plot was fully planned in advance. Or I can say it this way: this premeditated murder of John was fully plotted and planed out by Herodias. Instead of Herod and Herodias confessing and repenting of their sins, Herodias fully planned the details and then waited on the right day to implement the murder.

Well, it wasn't long until the day came with the perfect set of circumstances to implement John's murder. The best time was during Herod's birthday celebration, which was a grand festival for the ruler. Wine would be flowing freely, food would be in abundance, and of course, entertainment would be provided to please Herod's desires. The entertainment desires of Herod were lewd, sensual, and sexually exciting. This was Herod at his core. Lust drove him, and he proved how far he was willing to take his drive of lust with the marriage of Herodias. Now, Herodias would make sure this entertainment would be her opportunity to get what she wanted, John's death. She manipulated events for her daughter to be the main attraction at the birthday celebration, providing the right lewd entertainment. So, her strategy was to use wine, lust, and Herod's pride to overcome his hesitation about putting John to death.

> And when Herodias' daughter herself came in and danced . . . (Mark 6:22)

The plan was executed flawlessly down to the seductive lustfulness that seemed to overwhelm Herod's reasonable and rational thought processes to the point that he was willing to give away half of his kingdom!

> And when Herodias' daughter herself came in and danced, pleased Herod and those who sat with him, the king said to the girl, "Ask me whatever you want, and I will give it to you." He also swore to her, "Whatever you ask me, I will give you, up to half my kingdom." (Mark 6:22b–23)

Herodias daughter, Salome, didn't even know what to ask, she was so amazed and stunned at Herod's response. However, Herodias knew exactly what to tell her. Herodias had dreamed of this day, planned for this moment, and now she struck with a call for the death of John the Baptist.

> So she went out and said to her mother, "What shall I ask?" And she said, "The head of John the Baptist!" (Mark 6:24)

I think it is noteworthy to realize that it was very unusual for Salome to be dancing at this party at all. Not that lewd, sensual, and anything that could be considered licentious would be scheduled for Herod, but normally this dancing would be done by hired, professional harlots who were below the status of royal dignity. It certainly wouldn't be the daughter of Herodias; that would be below her status. But this would have made the show even more exciting for Herod, for anything from her would be taboo, and those evil of heart love to engage in these kinds of activities. So, Herod now is looking, lusting, and ready to take his wife's daughter! The perversions were accelerating.

> Immediately she came in with haste to the king and asked, saying, "I want you to give me at once the head of John the Baptist on a platter." And the king was exceedingly sorry; yet, because of the oaths and because of those who sat with him, he did not want to refuse her. Immediately the king sent an executioner and commanded his head to be brought. And he went and beheaded him in prison, brought his head on a platter, and gave it to the girl; and the girl gave it to her mother. (Mark 6:25–28)

Herod was manipulated by his wife to do the worst: to kill God's servant, John. He had sold himself to the evil appetites of the flesh and became vulnerable as a tool of the evil one. Herod could not control the lust of the flesh.

> But I discipline my body and bring it into subjection, lest, when I have preached to others, I myself should become disqualified. (1 Cor. 9:27)

Also, Herod had no real character to oppose this request. He could have just said no. Pick something else. He was king, but his pride would not allow him to say no to this request. His character had been developed over time and through his actions of the past. They had proven that lust and pride ruled Herod; Herod didn't rule them.

We must always remember that our character is developed over time and through our actions. Make sure you don't allow lust and pride to become your ruler. The Bible speaks to this:

> Do not love the world or the things in the world. If anyone loves the world, the love of the Father is not in him. For all that is in the world—the lust of the flesh, the lust of the eyes, and the pride of

life—is not of the Father but is of the world. And the world is passing away, and the lust of it; but he who does the will of God abides forever. (1 John 2:15–17)

To become a voice of fire means that sin will be revealed. Our goal is to simply preach the truth of God. This allows the Holy Spirit to direct this truth into the hearts of those who hear it. To some, this truth will pierce the soul, awaken the spirit, reveal sin, and put a call on them to repent and move in a new, godly direction. But understand this: for some people, it will turn them into a Herodias who will plot against you to harm your character or to shut down your voice. In other words, you will pay a high price for holy conduct. Just realize that this will come. Satan will plot, scheme, and desire to implement evil against you to shut down the voice of fire. John knew that he was stirring up hate with his preaching against Herod and Herodias, but he was a voice of fire and compelled by the Holy Spirit to keep preaching truth. John paid with his life! As voice of fire, preach the truth of God's holy Word and trust Him for the evil that will rise against you.

The Bible says to rejoice and be glad for your reward in heaven is great! So, rejoice as you become the target of attacks. This means that God is using you big-time for His kingdom. He also says fear not; God has this in His plan and purpose.

> And I say to you, My friends, do not be afraid of those who kill the body, and after that have no more that they can do. But I will show you whom you should fear: Fear Him who, after He has killed, has power to cast into hell; yes, I say to you, fear Him! Are not five sparrows sold for two copper coins? And not one of them is forgotten before God. But the very hairs of your head are all numbered. Do not fear therefore; you are of more value than many sparrows. (Luke 12:4–7)

God will never forget or forsake you! The most man can do is kill you—that's it! But God is the only one who can give eternal life and reward you for works done on this earth for His glory.

3. We Must Not Stumble over Things We Cannot Understand

We can't control the response of others to God's truth. Therefore, we will maintain a perspective of life that takes in more than our present situation. Today is not the end of the journey called life. Where is John the Baptist today? He is with the Lord Jesus Christ! John will be praised and remembered by all generations. He accomplished exactly what God called him to do. He was a voice of fire calling out for people to turn to God. So, where is Herod? He is experiencing the hot, burning flames of hell! Herod has all of eternity to be engulfed with his choice of flesh and self, ending in destruction.

Many times, God's will for our lives can be offensive to others. Preaching truth crosses our will and others, offending some. People certainly were offended with the teaching of Jesus.

> Is this not the carpenter, the Son of Mary, and brother of James, Joses, Judas, and Simon? And are not His sisters here with us?" So they were offended at Him. (Mark 6:3)

So, keep adding the logs of holy conduct. Let us love Him, serve Him, preach the truth, and be willing to take a stand for holy conduct, standing firm for truth, being courageous, and knowing that this is not the entirety of life. If you do this, I declare over you: *You will become a voice of fire!*

Preparation: Being Ready for Success

AS WE MOVE TOWARD BECOMING a voice of fire, one of the important logs are the steps required to prepare for God's success. Success here is not as the world defines it, but rather God's perfect timing aligning with the call in your life. Yes, there can be the call of God followed by a delay in the implementation or the execution of the actual follow through. One of the things I really want to stress is that there is an eternal reason for any time difference between the two.

I want to explore the life of a person I consider to be a voice of fire, Nehemiah, to underscore this truth. Nehemiah will always be especially associated with the rebuilding the wall in Jerusalem. It was this great and grand project which met with huge godly success that defines Nehemiah's purpose for the Lord. It is interesting that the Scriptures only cover about twelve years of Nehemiah's life. However, in those twelve years, Nehemiah left a huge imprint on history and made changes in Jerusalem that lasted for centuries.

The truth is: *It is not the length of time we have, but rather what we do with it.*

Nehemiah made the most of his time for the Lord, and we have so much we can learn for our souls through the life of Nehemiah.

Allow me to give some background that sets the stage for the success of God's purpose for Nehemiah. In 536 BC, many Jews were in captivity under Babylonian rule. Some Jews were allowed to return to Israel to reestablish a Jewish settlement, and some Jews actually escaped captivity. However, the conditions in Israel at this time were very bad. Nehemiah was still in captivity and was holding the position of cupbearer to the king. Now, understand, not just anyone could be a cupbearer. The king trusted his life in this man's faithful execution of this crucial role. Nehemiah had to be a person of outstanding character and completely trustworthy because he was to guard the king's person with his life. We should never discount the opportunities that good character and lifestyle can bring to our lives.

One day while serving in the king's palace, Nehemiah's brother came with some other men from Judah, and Nehemiah asked them about the Jewish settlement and about the condition of Jerusalem. His brother told him about the great misery and distress the people were in and the terrible condition of Jerusalem: the wall was broken down, and the gates were burned. In those days, broken down walls made the people vulnerable and easy prey to enemy invaders.

After Nehemiah learned about these terrible conditions in Israel, his heart was greatly burdened. In fact, he was so moved in his soul that he sat down and wept and went into mourning over the condition of Israel. The first thing Nehemiah did was to take his concerns to God in fasting and prayer.

As a voice of fire, the suffering of others should move our souls. So many today seem to have put this aspect of our Christianity aside. Those who have been called to be this voice of fire should have great compassion for the condition of people's lives, and prayer must be a common occurrence as circumstances unfold around us.

Preparation: Being Ready for Success

Understand: God has things in motion! God has a set of perfect circumstances, or another way to say it is, a God moment is coming! Many times, our realization of something does not always line up with His God moment. In Nehemiah's case, his prayer happened in the month of Chisley, or December, and four months went by before the God moment came to pass! Get this: God moments can take time to manifest. It is easy to begin to think nothing is going to happen, which can cause discouragement, promote pessimism, and be misinterpreted as God saying no. This kind of thought process can kill hope, discourage faith, and even make the heart sick.

Realize this truth: *Delays are not God saying no!*

God makes His answers to our prayers have the greatest impact and be the most profitable for His purpose. Remember, life has a lot of moving parts. God is at work, even shifting world events to answer our prayers! It took Mary and Joseph nine months to be in the right place at the right time for Jesus to be born where the prophecies declared He would be born! So, some delay is not God saying no.

Remember, delay can be of great value. This four-month delay gave Nehemiah time to prepare his plans to help Israel. It gave him time to prepare his speech before the king to ask for his release.

Here is something I really want you to see: *God's delays in responding to our prayers give us time to prepare for His answer.*

Truth is, when God delays a response, be patient and use that time to prepare for His answer. This is what a true voice of fire will do and thus reveal real faith while waiting for God's answer to our prayers. We must stay on the alert and be prepared in every situation to execute our plan as opportunities arise.

This is what happened to Nehemiah. His countenance was communicating his heart, and the king asked him this question: "Why is your face sad?" (Neh. 2:2). It was a very risky thing to be sad in front of the king; it was against the law. The king could have you killed just for a sad face! But Nehemiah could not hold back his heart, it was revealed in his face, and the king asked him about it. The timing was four months after Nehemiah's prayers, mourning and fasting, and his preparation to take action. This was now Nehemiah's opportunity to step up and share exactly and concisely what was on his heart. As a voice of fire, we must always be found standing ready to take action. Here, Nehemiah needs wisdom for this next question because his answer could cost him his life! So, notice how serious he takes it:

> Then the king said to me, "What do you request?" So I prayed to the God of heaven. (Neh. 2:4)

Nehemiah's next sentence was a prayer to the King of Kings! In an instant, before he made his request to the king on earth, he prayed to God in his heart and mind to help him answer. It was short, spontaneous, and silent but incredibly effective.

We Will Always Do Better Asking Men If We First Ask God

Nehemiah was fully prepared for success. He had planned what he wanted to ask the king, and he was able to communicate to him when God made the opportunity available. He sought God's help, courage, and wisdom for this very moment!

Let's look at Nehemiah's success together, understanding that as a voice of fire: *We must realize that success is not an accident.*

God is in control, period! As a voice of fire, we can never look at events as random circumstances that have no bearing on where we are, where we go, and what we do. Again, God is control. I believe we must submit to this by faith and as we do, nothing is an accident. The movement of people, world events, the orders of kings, and even the resistance of others, all are at work for our placement, purpose, and success as we serve the Lord.

And we know that all things work together for good to those who love God, to those who are the called according to His purpose. (Rom. 8:28)

So, let's agree with God on these truths:

1. Our Success Depends on Our God

Furthermore I said to the king, "If it pleases the king, let letters be given to me for the governors of the region beyond the River, that they must permit me to pass through till I come to Judah, and a letter to Asaph the keeper of the king's forest, that he must give me timber to make beams for the gates of the citadel which pertains to the temple, for the city wall, and for the house that I will occupy." And the king granted them to me according to the good hand of my God upon me. (Neh. 2:7–8)

"If it pleases the king" is very significant. If it did not please the king, it could be devastating! The relationship between the king and his subjects in those days was very different from any relationship we know about today. If angered in any way, the king could, and many times had, order one's death. So, someone approaching the king with a request must try very hard to form that request in a way that pleased him. However, in Nehemiah's case it was very hard to word this request in a positive or beneficial way to the king. This is the reason we *need* God! Pleasing the king can only come from God working his heart. Nehemiah's success to even begin on the journey to rebuild the wall started with God moving in the heart of the king. Without this intervention, no wall, no restoration of Israel, and perhaps even no more Nehemiah!

So, Nehemiah requested safe passage through the land and timber for the construction of the gates, temple, and his house all via a letter from the king. That's it. Well, that's almost it. Implied here is the leave of absence required for Nehemiah from the king's court and duties. It was not a small request due to the significance of his duty as cup bearer.

How does the king respond? By God's hand, the king was pleased! The king gave Nehemiah even more than he requested. The king granted him permission to rebuild the walls, temple, and house; appointed Nehemiah as governor of the province; and granted all the supplies requested plus what was needed for travel. He also gave him an extended leave of absence and sent an armed escort with him to make sure of his safety and that all others cooperated with him. He even allowed Nehemiah to set the duration of the leave of absence, which was twelve years. This was amazing! A king, ruler of the captured Jews, granting even more what than the captive asked—only God can do this kind of move on the heart of the king. Nehemiah understands this and says it this way:

> And the king granted them to me according to the good hand of my God upon me. (Neh. 2:8)

As a voice of fire, we must always give God the glory as He moves on our behalf. We have no success unless God causes it. None! The king here was only the agent of the true King. Always acknowledge all your success in ministry according to the good hand of your God upon you.

Let Us Be as Earnest in Our Glory to God as in Our Requests of God

Also, keep in mind the greatness of His power in us:

> Now to Him who is able to do exceedingly abundantly above all that we ask or think, according to the power that works in us. (Eph. 3:20)

2. Our Success Requires Us to Lay Groundwork

Success in God requires us to serve with impeccable character and faithfulness. Not only does this please God, but it also provides grounds for favor of man. God calls us to be at peace with all men. Nothing will lay this this type of groundwork like strong character and faithfulness to God. Nehemiah had served God and the king for many years with impeccable character and faithfulness, which demonstrates how groundwork paves the way for future successes in the work God has for us.

As a voice of fire, we should be in preparation for what God-given opportunities are coming. As we continue to prepare and then see God provide the very opportunity we prepared for, this shall fuel the fire to serve Him even more! The work of preparation is never a work wasted. In fact, the work of preparation is always rewarded as God sees and sends opportunities for us to use what we have prepared. As a voice of fire, always be preparing for success, remain faithful, and stand ready for God's timing. If so, I declare over you: *You will become a voice of fire!*

Prayer: The Heart and Soul

I BELIEVE THERE IS NOTHING more important than the fire log of prayer. Not just any prayer, but prayer with the understanding that things are accomplished by engaging the heavenlies on behalf of events on earth, prayer that is intense, prevailing, and binds over to earth what ought to be experienced here according to God's eternal will. Now, this is moving past the basic understanding that we ought to pray; the Bible and most godly teachers clearly teach us this truth. However, believers and voices of fire must move into a much deeper prayer life that actually targets and grips these items until a change of events on this earth takes place. Yes, it is possible for us to impact this earth through prayer! A voice of fire will move into the kind of prayer that wrestles with evil and agrees with God's purposes and plans for good in order to see it implemented on earth. Many times, people push back about having this great privilege of prayer and the significant power it engages. May God speak as you read and think about this part of keeping the fire burning!

So, let's agree on the basic truth that all prayer is a great privilege to all believers with many aspects.

Many also believe that prayer and supplication are the same thing. That is not so. There is a difference in these two aspects.

> Praying always with all prayer and supplication in the Spirit, being watchful to this end with all perseverance and supplication for all the saints. (Eph. 6:18)

I define prayer as being earnest, diligent, and fervent in asking of the Lord to provide, to give us wisdom, and to lead our lives. This is how we so often find ourselves when we pray alone, with friends, or at prayer meetings. The focus of this prayer is on God helping us through difficult circumstances, provision in times of need, or our great need for guidance and/or direction. The Bible certainly calls us to ask for these things:

> Ask, and it will be given to you; seek, and you will find; knock, and it will be opened to you. For everyone who asks receives, and he who seeks finds, and to him who knocks it will be opened. (Matt. 7:7–8)

So, it is right that we should ask and expect to receive. God is declaring it is right to ask and promises that He hears and answers prayers. The issue is not these kinds of prayers. The point I am making is considering that prayers and supplications are the same. They are not, but many times in the Scripture, we find these two words linked together. So, let's look at the idea of supplication.

The Greek word for supplication, is *deesis*, which is defined as prayer that focuses on the manifestation of God's victorious purpose. Let's look at three biblical usages of deesis.

1. The Call for a Release of God-Created Order

Supplication calls for God-intended life, initially designed to be released, to come forth. Just one example of this was Zacharias' supplication that his barren wife be blessed with a child.

> But the angel said to him, "Do not be afraid, Zacharias, for your prayer [deesis] is heard; and your wife Elizabeth will bear you a son, and you shall call his name John. (Luke 1:13)

Here, supplication made by Zacharias is for the normal, God-designed, creative reproduction process to be released into his wife, Elizabeth. God sends an angel to give Zacharias a message that God is reversing the hindrance on Elizabeth, and He will release His created order.

Zacharias, through supplications, calls for God's created order to be manifested in their circumstances, and God moved events on earth to give Zacharias and Elizabeth a child. Zacharias simply called for this alignment of God's creative will and for it to be done on earth as it is in heaven.

> Your kingdom come. Your will be done on earth as it is in heaven. (Matt. 6:10)

Glory to God!

2. The Call for an Intervention by God for Others

This supplication is a sincere, regular, and relentless one that does not give up until God's answer is given. An example of this would be the supplication by the church in Philippi for the release of Paul from a Roman prison.

> For I know that this will turn out for my deliverance through your prayer [deesis] and the supply of the Spirit of Jesus Christ. (Phil. 1:19)

Here, supplication is being made by the church on behalf of Paul's circumstances in Rome. The Philippian church was sincerely and relentlessly calling for God's release of His servant Paul from a Roman prison. So, through supplication, they were calling for God to intervene on behalf of Paul, to change the circumstances, and to release him from prison.

3. The Call for Success in Kingdom Work

This is an intense, spiritual fight for the entirety of God's kingdom to triumph on earth. The Scriptures clearly calls us to pray this way,

> Praying always with all prayer and supplication in the Spirit. (Eph. 6:18)

Now, we must look at the context of this great call to prayer and supplication to fully understand the meaning. The context of verse 18 is within the Scripture that calls us to,

> Therefore take up the whole armor of God, that you may be able to withstand in the evil day, and having done all, to stand. (Eph. 6:13)

This contextual understanding brings powerful meaning to what we are praying to support. The call is to take up the full armor of God because we are in a fight, and we will need the armor of God to see victory for the army of God! Therefore, the command of supplication caps off the whole instruction on being properly armed to bring triumph on earth. So, in this context, we are commanded to be praying (deesis) always for all the saints to be victorious in the battle against the wiles of the devil! Also, Paul gives a very specific request that he may be given the words to say to communicate the mystery of the gospel. In other words, Paul is asking for supplication (deesis) to be made for the success of the gospel as he shares it with the world!

Therefore, supplications are pleas for God's ordained, perfect will to appear here and now. And by this, He shall triumph above any and all earthly powers that resist Him, and He shall overthrow all of the principalities, powers, rulers of the darkness of this age, spiritual hosts of wickedness, and anything and anyone who stands against God Almighty!

So, what is the ultimate supplication example? We find it recorded in Hebrews:

> Who, in the days of His flesh, when He had offered up prayers and supplications, with vehement cries and tears to Him who was able to save Him from death, and was heard because of His godly fear, though He was a Son, yet He learned obedience by the things which He suffered. And having been perfected, He became the author of eternal salvation to all who obey Him. (Heb. 5:7–9)

Jesus Christ was the ultimate example of supplication. Truth is, it took God stepping into man's dimension as His perfect plan, His prayers and supplication, and His own suffering and death to solve the infinitely complex entanglement of our lives in sin! The Holy Spirit has given this Scripture to remind us that it was in the days of our Lord Jesus Christ's flesh, the days that He walked on this earth, that the nature and fact of Jesus' supplication helped bring about God's perfect plan for mankind. The pinnacle of this supplication is found in the garden of Gethsemane when Jesus Christ, the man, pleaded,

> Father, if it is Your will, take this cup away from Me; nevertheless not My will, but Yours, be done. (Luke 22:42)

Christ was in full knowledge of the agony He would face in the coming days on the journey to the cross. He knew about the beatings, mockings, and even the brutal death He would face. However, even with this knowledge, through supplication, He called for the divine; he needed action by God for His purpose to be accomplished for eternity. Jesus Christ settled with, "nevertheless not My will, but Yours, be done." The truth is, without the shedding of the blood of the Lamb, there would be no remission of sin. The Bible is clear as to God's perfect plan for mankind:

> Christ was offered once to bear the sins of many. To those who eagerly wait for Him He will appear a second time, apart from sin, for salvation. (Heb. 9:28)

All of this was decided in the councils of the Holy Trinity before the world and man were created. Jesus Christ agreed to this solution for mankind's sin problem and God's eternity solution. And it is clear, supplication helped to accomplish this amazing will of God, born before the world was even created. Supplication was offered through the travail of tears, the trail of blood from Gethsemane to the cross, and the profound suffering of the cross. All of God's purpose was called forth through supplication from Christ Himself. By any definition, this was *success for kingdom work*. Hallelujah!

Supplications Are Prayers That Change the Events of Earth According to the Creative Will of God

So, through supplications, we are to agree with God's perfect will and ask for its manifestation, we are to ask for His divine purpose to be revealed clearly, and we are to pray relentlessly, knowing that through our supplications, events on this earth can be dramatically and significantly changed. Voices of fire will engage the heavenlies with relentless, prevailing, and believing supplications by faith that God shall move!

Are you ready to pray for a release of God's created order, for an intervention by God, and His success in kingdom work? If you are, I declare over you: *You will become a voice of fire!*

Voices of Fire Shall Engage the Heavenlies with Our Supplications

Supplication will be that intense, prevailing prayer form that calls forth on earth what ought to be experienced here according to God's eternal counsels.

The next aspect I would like to address about prayer is from our distinct perspective of one asking boldly because God invites us to do so!

Let's start with: *Ask boldly of God.*

> The effective, fervent prayer of a righteous man avails much. (James 5:16)

The context of this passage is powerful. It includes the context of believers and everyday Christians. It begins with, "Is anyone among you suffering? Let him pray" (James 5:13). It then continues with other examples of prayer and re-enforces that God will answer your prayers! That's right, the Scriptures are encouraging you to pray and see things changed by the power of God!

So, we conclude: *Prayer is a pathway that anyone can walk.*

Again, this is underscored in the same passage as it moves into a personal example of Elijah.

> Elijah was a man with a nature like ours, and he prayed earnestly that it would not rain; and it did not rain on the land for three years and six months. And he prayed again, and the heaven gave rain, and the earth produced its fruit. (James 5:17–18)

Here, the Scriptures tell us that Elijah, being just a man with the same struggles and sins we wrestle with, prayed earnestly that it would not rain, and it did not rain. Then, after three years and six months, he prayed for rain, and it rained. Therefore, even this personal example supports the truth that we can engage in prayer, and God will hear from heaven and answer. The rub comes with what does the fervent prayer of a righteous man mean. Some would say you must be full of the Holy Spirit as demonstrated by a certain gift. Others would say you must be very religious and follow a certain set of rules that obviously makes you "righteous." I believe that Scripture is calling all believers who stand in the imputed righteousness of our Lord Jesus Christ, to pray earnestly and ask God for that which will reverse the curse of evil in our land. The promise here in Scripture is that God will answer our prayers. How bold was Elijah in asking God to stop the rain for three and one half years?

This leads us to this amazing truth: *We are to ask of God freely and boldly for whatever we need.*

Let me share with you what I believe should be the foundational attitude of prayer. After Jesus finished teaching the disciples how to pray, He shared this story and instruction on prayer:

> Which of you shall have a friend, and go to him at midnight and say to him, "Friend, lend me three loaves; for a friend of mine has come to me on his journey, and I have nothing to set before him;" and he will answer from within and say, "Do not trouble me; the door is now shut, and my children are with me in bed; I cannot rise and give to you?" I say to you, though he will not rise and give to him because he is his friend, yet because of his persistence he will rise and give him as many as he needs. So I say to you, ask, and it will be given to you; seek, and you will find; knock, and it will be opened to you. For everyone who asks receives, and he who seeks finds, and to him who knocks it will be opened. If a son asks for bread from any father among you, will he give him a stone? Or if he asks for a fish, will he

give him a serpent instead of a fish? Or if he asks for an egg, will he offer him a scorpion? If you then, being evil, know how to give good gifts to your children, how much more will your heavenly Father give the Holy Spirit to those who ask Him! (Luke 11:5–13)

I believe, in general, Jesus is saying that we are to ask both freely and boldly for whatever we need with no hesitation at all. Jesus is saying, "Answer me this: which of you has a friend who would stand at his bedroom window and shout out to you, 'Don't bother me! Everyone is in bed?'" The answer is clear: of course he would not! This is not even about friendship as much as it is about what He would give to you to meet your needs because of the simple fact that you have the boldness to ask. Jesus underscores this with, "So I say to you, ask, and it will be given to you." This leads us to three foundational attitudes about prayer that will add effectiveness to our prayers.

1. We Must Have the Spiritual Nerve to Ask Boldly

It must be understood that our Father will listen to our prayers at any time. The problem is with us. We must let go of any fear or hang-ups that keep us from asking of the Father. If we understand that the Father has granted us access to Him at any time, then we must learn to have the boldness to ask of Him freely.

Go to him at midnight and say to him. (Luke 11:5)

Jesus encourages us to become a person who is so aware of the need that we are willing to abandon normal protocols and approach others with singleness of mind to ask for our needs to be met

What is the promise? It is clear: the awakened friend gets up and gives whatever is needed. This is what our Father in heaven will also do!

2. We Must Overcome Our Hesitation to Ask Freely

Freely means ceaseless petitioning. *Ask*, here, is in a verb form and conveys the condition of continual asking. In other words, you never need to hesitate to ask of the Father just because you asked Him earlier. God never gets too busy with your earlier requests to listen and provide for new ones. We must never hesitate to ask of God. Period.

3. We Must Not Be Afraid to Ask for Anything

Jesus is telling us that the problem is not with God but with our hesitance to ask. Whatever our circumstance or need, ask with boldness. To a point, He offers us a blank check within His will to ask whatever we want that He may give it to us. Because we don't know or understand the total will of God, we should err on the side of boldly asking often.

> You did not choose Me, but I chose you and appointed you that you should go and bear fruit, and that your fruit should remain, that whatever you ask the Father in My name He may give you. (John 15:16)

Voices of fire will boldly ask of the Father. They will repeatedly, fervently, and persistently ask of God according to the need. The idea of a bold, continual asking and ceaseless petitioning for the necessary requirements as we serve our God is encouraged by Jesus Christ and the Word of God. Our Father will answer and give to us! If you are willing to boldly ask of Him, I declare over you: *You will become a voice of fire!*

Prayer That Restores

The final aspect I would like to address about prayer is from the perspective that prayer can restore what the enemy has taken. Let's start with:

Prayer: The Heart and Soul

> For though we walk in the flesh, we do not war according to the flesh. For the weapons of our warfare are not carnal but mighty in God for pulling down strongholds, casting down arguments and every high thing that exalts itself against the knowledge of God, bringing every thought into captivity to the obedience of Christ. (2 Cor. 10:3–5)

Keep in mind that our enemy's role involves wave after wave of attacks and chaos cast against God and His people. These certainly include, but are not limited to, boastings against God, lying to the created, blaming God for our problems, hurting as many people as possible, constant indictments against mankind that cause further distress, guilt, condemnation, bitterness, and ultimately destruction in some form. The Bible tells us this about the enemy:

> The thief does not come except to steal, and to kill, and to destroy. I have come that they may have life, and that they may have it more abundantly. (John 10:10)

As believers, we must remember that we possess, on the tip of our tongues, the answer to all the adversary's charges, no matter the accusation. Many seem to be out of touch or confused about this. I think it is because much of this drama takes place in the spiritual dimension, or what we call the spiritual realm, that we cannot see or touch or even feel as we go through our walks in Christ. The only way we can is if Christ Himself opens a window of insight for us to see this spiritual dimension clearly. So many times, this lack of seeing or understanding leads to us dealing with the symptoms rather than addressing the root causes—or dealing with the problem rather than the source.

Many get stuck in the never-ending cycle of irritation, frustration, complaining, or confusion about the problem altogether. They aimlessly move from day-to-day in a fog, not knowing what to do about it all. Even when they pray (the right action to take in this kind of warfare), they rarely come close to the mark of the real problem. Perhaps they pray out of a desperation of the enemies working, rather than joining together with the Holy Spirit to declare the enemy's total, unadulterated destruction. I think the basic problem here is so many act as though they are unaware of the schemes of the evil one.

> Be sober, be vigilant; because your adversary the devil walks about like a roaring lion, seeking whom he may devour. Resist him, steadfast in the faith, knowing that the same sufferings are experienced by your brotherhood in the world. (1 Peter 5:8–9)

I see Christians in their everyday walk who act as though they are victims and are clueless to the schemes and tactics of Satan. But even if they are aware, their reaction times are too slow to deploy weapons that disrupt his operations against them. The great news is that the real conclusion is yet to be played out by those who are willing and who will learn to shape events through prayer.

Christ commissioned His disciples, including us as believers:

> Also He said to them, "In whatever place you enter a house, stay there till you depart from that place. And whoever will not receive you nor hear you, when you depart from there, shake off the dust under your feet as a testimony against them. Assuredly, I say to you, it will be more tolerable for Sodom and Gomorrah in the day of judgment than for that city!" So they went out and preached that people should repent. And they cast out many demons, and anointed with oil many who were sick, and healed them. (Mark 6:10–13)

These disciples were the tip of the spear. They had the task to take the gospel to people and reverse the progress of the evil one. It would require faith for sure, but it would also require fervent, powerful prayers that would restore what the enemy had taken. So, the lives the enemy had possessed were to be set free or be restored. Who the enemy had caused to be sick were to be healed or restored. Judgement would be stayed on the homes that received the message of the gospel by the time the disciples left. In other words, God's creative order would have been restored for these people! So, the question is this: how is this power invoked to change world events? One obvious way that I believe doesn't need much comment is through the power of the Holy Spirit. No question: prayer that restores is undoable apart from God Almighty's power engaged in every situation, sickness, healing, and salvation. But I also believe that much does not happen without intercessory prayer. It is incumbent on us to be disciplined and to remain as in tune with the Holy Spirit as possible to maximize God's deliverance upon this earth. Intercessory prayer can and does restore God's place where the enemy has invaded or possessed. In fact, our intercessory prayers can influence world events and people events where evil has made its mark. Therefore, this leads me to expound on prayer that restores what the enemy has taken.

I really want this truth to sink into our hearts: *Our intercession will impact human events.*

I see human events that are subject to be altered right now! That's right; prayer that restores can alter the events on the ground right now. However, for restoration to take place, God has decided that we must be engaged in earnest, intercessory prayer. It reminds me of a time in the Scriptures when the church of the living God was in earnest, intercessory prayer for Peter who was in prison under heavy guard. Let's look at this Scripture:

> Peter was therefore kept in prison, but constant prayer was offered to God for him by the church. . . . Now behold, an angel of the Lord stood by him, and a light shone in the prison; and he struck Peter on the side and raised him up, saying, "Arise quickly!" And his chains fell off his hands. Then the angel said to him, "Gird yourself and tie on your sandals"; and so he did. And he said to him, "Put on your

garment and follow me." So he went out and followed him, and did not know that what was done by the angel was real, but thought he was seeing a vision. When they were past the first and the second guard posts, they came to the iron gate that leads to the city, which opened to them of its own accord; and they went out and went down one street, and immediately the angel departed from him. And when Peter had come to himself, he said, "Now I know for certain that the Lord has sent His angel, and has delivered me from the hand of Herod and from all the expectation of the Jewish people." So, when he had considered this, he came to the house of Mary, the mother of John whose surname was Mark, where many were gathered together praying. And as Peter knocked at the door of the gate, a girl named Rhoda came to answer. When she recognized Peter's voice, because of her gladness she did not open the gate, but ran in and announced that Peter stood before the gate. But they said to her, "You are beside yourself!" Yet she kept insisting that it was so. So they said, "It is his angel." Now Peter continued knocking; and when they opened the door and saw him, they were astonished. (Acts 12:5, 7–16)

Now, take notice, it is not as if these believers had such great faith that they somehow, by faith, just made this happen. Not at all. These believers came together and put forth fervent, intercessory prayers for Peter, a dear brother, who was imprisoned, and they needed him. They called forth, by prayer, the Father's will, and Peter was miraculously released. They were used, through their prayers, to alter the events of Peter's life and the events of all time. Wow! Think about this. Fervent, intercessory prayer of the saints was used by God to completely alter the events for Peter as he led the church and to record it in Scripture for all to come, namely you and me. Again, their faith was so little that when Peter showed up, they did not even believe it. But God, full of mercy and grace says clearly:

If you have faith as a mustard seed, you will say to this mountain, "Move from here to there," and it will move; and nothing will be impossible for you. (Matt. 17:20)

So, if you can believe that our intercession will impact human events, I declare over you: *You will become a voice of fire!* But this is not all!

Our Intercession Will Impact the Spiritual Dimension

Intercession is a strategic, powerful weapon to be used for the redemption of mankind. This is why the enemy works overtime to keep people of God from coming together to pray in any form. He knows that the redeemed can restore what progress he has made in lives, relationships, and the church. If the church today realized the restoring power that intercessory prayer possesses, prayer night would be the most attended meeting of the church. The church has lost its desire to see the power of God move in the spiritual dimension on behalf of the lost lives within the church and much less so in the world. To be a voice of fire, this is unacceptable! Pushing back and ultimately restoring God's perfect will in an event on earth and in the spiritual dimension is the heartbeat of a voice of fire. So, let's look at three areas this impacts:

1. A Relationship with God

> Therefore He is also able to save to the uttermost those who come to God through Him, since He always lives to make intercession for them. (Heb. 7:25)

God will save family, friends, and even the people of the world to the uttermost. Christ lives to make intercession for them. This is the will of God. It is what we should intercede for at all times. In this we can change human events and spiritual events for those who will be saved. What is wrong with us? Are we so secure that we don't even care enough to intercede for those who are lost? Voices of fire will intercede for the soul who needs salvation and pray that Christ would save them to the uttermost!

2. The Working of the Holy Spirit in Our Lives

> Likewise the Spirit also helps in our weaknesses. For we do not know what we should pray for as we ought, but the Spirit Himself makes intercession for us with groanings which cannot be uttered. Now He who searches the hearts knows what the mind of the Spirit is, because He makes intercession for the saints according to the will of God. (Rom. 8:26–27)

We intercede knowing that we can't possibly know everything we ought to pray; however, God the Holy Spirit certainly does understand exactly what to pray and will intercede for us so that everything necessary is called forth. Yes, it is all accomplished according to the will of God. We are not alone to press into the spiritual dimension and expected to get it just right. We are called into an earnest, fervent intercessory prayer, asking for the will of God to be done. God the Holy Spirit is right there with us, making sure any and all things are called forth.

3. The Influence of the Church on Society

> Therefore I exhort first of all that supplications, prayers, intercessions, and giving of thanks be made for all men, for kings and all who are in authority, that we may lead a quiet and peaceable life in all godliness and reverence. For this is good and acceptable in the sight of God our Savior, who desires all men to be saved and to come to the knowledge of the truth. (1 Tim. 2:1–4)

These verses reveal that intercession directly affects what happens between people. It can be God and man, mankind and mankind, or mankind with nations; whomever it is, the message is clear. Our intercession has an altering influence in each of these. Intercession is way more than asking for something; it is actually engaging in the opportunity God has given us to be part of the influence on the possible outcomes.

This is the kind of prayer that engages the heavenlies and restores our territory. Voices of fire desire this kind of engagement with God and others.

So, our big challenge is: *Restore territory through intercessory prayer.*

The way we look at intercessory prayer is very important. I see it in two ways. The first is entering into a partnership in God's operation to rescue mankind. Without intercession, hell can break in like a flood after the dam breaks, flooding everything in its path with total destruction. Second, it is a partnership to restore God's original territory in my life and the church—where Satan has intruded upon what God intended as joy for individuals, invaded God's boundaries, and where he has encroached upon our lives. We can push the adversary back and reverse the curse of his progress. Intercession can redo the border lines and reinstate them to the proper dimensions, restoring our territories. Voices of fire will use prayer to reach into the dimensions of God's destiny for any situation and call forth total restoration. Are you ready to reach in and call forth? If you are, I declare over you: *You will become a voice of fire!*

> He delivered me from my strong enemy,
> From those who hated me,
> For they were too strong for me.
> They confronted me in the day of my calamity,
> But the Lord was my support.
> He also brought me out into a broad place;
> He delivered me because He delighted in me. (Ps. 18:17–19)

Perspective: Heavenly Vision

TRUTH IS, IN LIFE AND in business, we are much more impactful and effective if we have set goals and work toward those goals. In business, there are many goals, ranging from each individual worker to the highest-level CEO. Most business plans range from the current year to a five-year plan, for we know that without goals, businesses will end up producing chaotic results and not be most effective with their resources. Also, it has been proven that people who set goals and focus on those goals in their individual lives, will achieve much more than those who do not set clear goals for themselves. The issue is not if this is right or not. The issue is if we are so good in setting goals in business and perhaps even in our own personal lives, why don't we have clear and understood spiritual goals, and why aren't we pressing for them?

A very large percentage of Christians today do not seem to understand the importance of setting goals to become most effective for the kingdom of God. This perspective has lost its luster in today's Christian community. There seems to be little appetite for serious, thoughtful, challenging goal-setting within the Christian community. Oh, we see what I would call small, focused goals or inadequate attempts to check this box sometimes, but mostly the focus is on our giving goals so that we make our declared budgets within the church. Nothing wrong with this in itself, but where is the perspective that says we desire to be the best and most we can be for the Lord Jesus Christ this year and even five years out? Where is the desire to set challenging personal goals to know Him more, engage in intercessory prayer, to minister to others, to give more to support the gospel all over the world, and to press on in walking in His ways? These also should be looked at, and we should keep right perspective monthly to evaluate our progress and be assessed by the voice of the Holy Spirit as we press on toward them.

Think about this with me for a moment as I look at what it would take to achieve a gold medal in the Olympics. What kind of commitment is involved? What would it take to achieve this honored medal? For sure, it would take keeping the eye on the goal. Only one individual for every six million plus people on the planet will achieve the goal of winning the gold medal at the Olympics. Besides the obvious advantage of the God-given ability to run, jump, or anything else the athlete works for, what does it require? Every gold medalist will tell you that it requires mental focus on the goal and hours and hours of training and preparation every day for years and years. It takes mental toughness, guts, and determination to push a body that has reached its limits and even more to fight through the physical pain to become victorious over other rivals.

So, the gold medal path requires a talent to be recognized, nurtured, harnessed, and channeled to rest in the absolute winning strategy that will be victorious over all comers. This up-coming talent will need a coach, infrastructure, equipment, and facilities that also commits to the support of this individual.

When an individual wins a gold medal, the prize is significant. They receive compensation from their government and huge financial corporate sponsorships that could easily reach ten million dollars. So, if you become the one in six million people who achieve the goal of obtaining an Olympic gold medal, the prize is very profitable. OK, so it is clear that very few individuals make it to the Olympics gold medal platform or to the amazing prestige given to those who actually reach their goal.

As God's possession, the Word of God calls us to be seriously committed to the prize.

> Not that I have already attained, or am already perfected; but I press on, that I may lay hold of that for which Christ Jesus has also laid hold of me. Brethren, I do not count myself to have apprehended; but one thing I do, forgetting those things which are behind and reaching forward to those things which are ahead, I press toward the goal for the prize of the upward call of God in Christ Jesus. (Phil. 3:12–14)

So that leads us to this truth: *God calls His people to be committed to the prize.*

I think the first question is: are you a Christian who is fully committed to the prize God is talking about in Philippians? Are your goals established, and can progress be measured toward them? Do they reflect that you are a person with a serious commitment to His prize? How would you answer these questions? Would you say, "What prize?" Or would you even resist in some way, saying, "I don't make commitments"? Or perhaps you don't understand or don't even know what the prize Paul is referring to within this passage.

A clear definition of the prize is a good way to begin. It can be best defined in several different promises of God through the Scriptures.

The first is the promise of ultimate, eternal salvation in God's kingdom. The Bible tells us that one of the aspects of the prize is found in the wonderful redemption of sinful man by a holy God! This is the most important part of this prize. To think that a holy God would care so much about sinful mankind that He would provide the only way to be redeemed—by the blood of Jesus Christ our Lord and Savior!

This is revealed in so many places in Scripture and certainly is a prize possession of believers.

> In Him we have redemption through His blood, the forgiveness of sins, according to the riches of His grace which He made to abound toward us in all wisdom and prudence, having made known to us the mystery of His will . . . In Him you also trusted, after you heard the word of truth, the gospel of your salvation; in whom also, having believed, you were sealed with the Holy Spirit of promise, who is the guarantee of our inheritance until the redemption of the purchased possession, to the praise of His glory. (Eph. 1:7–9, 13–14)

Second, the promise of heaven itself is an aspect of the prize. Heaven is a real place just as much as your hometown. It's sad to say, many people today believe they are going to heaven when they die without knowing for sure according to Scripture. They answer the question about going to heaven with, "I hope so," or "I think so," or "I think I've got a good chance," i.e. "Me and the man upstairs have a good understanding!" Truth is, heaven is forever, and each person needs to know for sure where they are going. If they are wrong, it will be for all of eternity.

Heaven is God's dwelling place where Christ sits at the right hand of the Father. Heaven can be referred to by believers as our Father's house.

> Let not your heart be troubled; you believe in God, believe also in Me. In My Father's house are many mansions; if it were not so, I would have told you. I go to prepare a place for you. And if I go and prepare a place for you, I will come again and receive you to Myself; that where I am, there you may be also. (John 14:1–3)

In our Father's house, He is preparing a place for all who come to Him! That, my friend, is a great aspect of the prize!

The Bible not only calls heaven God's dwelling place but also paradise. Paradise was used by Christ while on the cross as he speaks to the forgiven criminal. Jesus said:

> Assuredly, I say to you, today you will be with Me in Paradise. (Luke 23:43)

The idea of paradise is delight, glory, joy, and bliss. So, to be with Him in heaven or paradise will be to experience the greatest joy possible. In fact, the Bible tells us we shall be like Him! This is the greatest aspect of our prize to come.

The amazing view of heaven revealed in Scripture continues in Revelation. It says heaven is a place where God will wipe away every tear; there will be no more sickness or pain; no more sorrow, crying, or mourning, not even any death; no more hunger or thirst; and no more violence or wars ever again! We are talking about perfect peace forever and forever. Again, this is another wonderful aspect of the prize.

Heaven is also a place where we shall receive our rewards at the judgment seat of Christ.

> Now if anyone builds on this foundation with gold, silver, precious stones, wood, hay, straw, each one's work will become clear; for the Day will declare it, because it will be revealed by fire; and the fire will test each one's work, of what sort it is. If anyone's work which he has built on it endures, he will receive a reward. If anyone's work is burned, he will suffer loss; but he himself will be saved, yet so as through fire. (1 Cor. 3:12–15)

Heaven is a picture of never growing old, never any sadness, never any pain, and never any conflict. Heaven is a place where we will worship without distraction, serve without exhaustion, fellowship without fear, learn without fatigue, and rest without boredom! It is clear to me that heaven is a piece of the prize we are talking about.

Paul exhorts us to set a focus on the prize! Certainly, the prize includes the promise of ultimate, eternal salvation and heaven itself. If we make sure we define the prize that God desires us to place our focus and energy on, then we can begin to place our uncompromising commitment to this prize. We can set goals to position ourselves to maximize our lives for the Lord Jesus Christ while on earth with a focus and right perspective that this world is not our home.

> For our citizenship is in heaven, from which we also eagerly wait for the Savior, the Lord Jesus Christ, who will transform our lowly body that it may be conformed to His glorious body, according to the working by which He is able even to subdue all things to Himself. (Phil. 3:20–21)

The right perspective is very important to help keep us focused for the days to come and to be used of God to the fullest. A voice of fire will keep the right perspective on where their home really is, which is heaven to come. We are on a journey on this earth that is only temporal, short lived, and then our eternity will be staring us right in our face. The only perspective then that will matter will be our relationship with Christ and what was done with the right heart on this earth for the kingdom!

Five Right Perspectives to Remain Committed to the Prize

1. Realize Our Humanity

   Not that I have already attained, or am already perfected. (Phil. 3:12)

   Paul's conversion was thirty years prior to this point in his life. He had won many spiritual battles, planted many churches, raised up

Perspective: Heavenly Vision

preachers and teachers, discipled many, and traveled long missionary journeys. He was struck blind by Christ, and a man laid hands on him so he could receive his sight; he was shipwrecked, beaten to death, and was brought back to life; he was used by God in many ways, testifying before kings, rulers, and religious leaders, healing many people just by his shadow passing over them; and so much more. Now, why do I list all these things of Paul? Because when we realize how much he was tested, how many trials he endured, and the sheer volume of ministry he accomplished, in our eyes, it would have been easy for him to boast, saying perhaps, "Look at what I have done," or even, "I have arrived in my knowledge and service to the Lord." But he didn't say this at all. Paul said, "I have not arrived at all, nor am I perfect at all!" Paul realized his sinful, weak humanity. He understood that no one will be where they need to be until they see Christ. We must always keep this perspective. We have not already attained or are already perfected.

If we ever stop seeking to grow, we begin to wither. We must fight against the evil-inspired spiritual plateaus beyond which we cannot climb. We cannot ever allow a stalemate in our spiritual growth; it is the work of the enemy. Always carry the right perspective that we all are in process, that none of us have arrived at every answer or the highest spiritual level, and that we have failed in the past and will fail again. Sin is still something we wrestle with every day, and we are challenged with sin as we live our Christians lives. The right perspective is clear; we have not already attained or are already perfected. A voice of fire will realize our humanity, as Paul did, no matter how much God seems to use us.

2. Remain Single Minded

> But one thing I do. (Phil 3:13)

There is a great need for all of us to remain focused on what is important. Today our lives are filled with too many things that really do not matter. We must prioritize according to what is significant to our spiritual growth that will really count for the glory of God and see to it that this is the one thing we do to see these things come to pass.

The right perspective is clear. The one thing we do is to make a commitment to being single-minded. This will cause us to grow, be, live, and serve our God in a way that He would have us to serve. A voice of fire will realize that single-mindedness is for their good, and this will help block out the distraction the enemy will always bring into our way.

3. Letting Go of the Past

Forgetting those things which are behind. (Phil 3:13)

It is high time that Christians from all walks of life let go of the past. It is time to unpack your suitcase of carnal baggage—ungodliness, wrong-thinking, complaining, doubt, and fear—and totally repack it with only those things that will support you being what God desires you to be. Don't allow Satan to bring up the past to derail your walk in the Lord. He will try to remind you of every failure and wrong turn and condemn your heart because of past things. He is a liar and a thief, trying to manipulate your view of yourself in Christ. You do not have to allow your past to control you! Paul was a persecutor of Christians and even a murderer, yet he was forgiven and his sins forgotten by God. If God has forgotten our past, why can't we forget it? The past is behind us, and God is telling us to let go. The right perspective is clear; we should forget those things which are behind, those things causing us to fail, quit, or be filled with doubt and unbelief. A voice of fire will realize that letting go of the past is for their good, and this will help us move deeper into our amazing relationship with Christ, setting us free to serve Him to the fullest!

4. Reaching Forward

Reaching forward to those things which are ahead. (Phil. 3:13)

I believe this is reaching forward to the hope of our future, desiring more and more in Him. Paul pursued Christlikeness with enthusiasm and persistence exactly like an Olympic gold medalist. He was willing to do everything it would take. He was found reaching for those things that are ahead in Christ. The right perspective is clear; we are to reach forward. God has a future and a plan for our lives, and it is a good plan! A voice of fire will realize that reaching forward is the only way we will ever arrive at what God wants us to be.

5. Knowing the Goal for the Prize

I press toward the goal for the prize. (Phil 3:14)

It is also very clear that God desires us to know Him more. Not to just know *of* Him, by the hearing of the ear but to know Him and have a blessed, eye-opening experience that says, "Now my eyes see You, oh God!" Once you have tasted this experience, you then set your desire to press on toward the prize of the upward call of God in Christ Jesus. Pressing on toward the goal includes being determined with great concentration and vigorously seeking to know Him. The right perspective is that we know the goal for the prize and are willing to press on to obtain it. God has a wonderful prize coming for you. A voice of fire will realize that knowing the goal is fundamental to our steadfastness and faithfulness to our walk in Christ. It is critical to our pressing on in Christ Jesus our Lord. This is being committed to the prize. What do we find ourselves committed to today? Jobs, sports, hobbies, or friends? When we seek Him with all of our being, we have the right perspective. Do you press on for the right perspective in all things? If you do, I declare over you: *You will become a voice of fire!*

12

Perseverance: Ride the Wave

IN MINISTRY, THERE WILL BE ups and downs, wins and losses, cause and effect, answered prayers, and the fallout from those answers. I call this the waves of ministry. Anyone who engages in ministry in any way must be ready to ride these waves. Much like a ship at sea, we must ride the wave up and then ride it down in order to move through the sea to our destination.

During any ministry, there will be a starting point, then building, adding to the numbers, and expansion. This is riding the wave up. There likewise can be many things that happen to cause us to contract in ministry. I call this riding the wave down. For an example, someone may be called to begin another ministry. They will have others who are connected to them and many may follow them, reducing and creating a void in the current ministry. Not all the ups and downs are exactly what I have just described, but I only share these two as examples of riding the waves to help you get the picture of what I am talking about. There will be both the feeling of riding up and riding down in ministry!

Now, I believe many people of faith, of prayer, of obedience, and of service to God have seen these ministry waves. Paul had to ride them many times. Peter rode them. Abraham was found dealing with them. So, great people of God have experienced them. Thus, we will be in great company along our ride. I want us to look at a specific example of how a great man of faith rode the waves of ministry, namely Elijah.

Elijah came on the scene when Ahab was king over Israel. Ahab was the eighth king of Israel and the Bible describes him this way:

> And Ahab made a wooden image. Ahab did more to provoke the Lord God of Israel to anger than all the kings of Israel who were before him. (1 Kings 16:33)

Ahab did significant evil in the sight of the Lord, more than all the kings before him. Ahab ushered in Baal worship and service into Israel. In fact, Baal worship and service became widespread in Israel during the reign of Ahab. Baal was considered to be the most powerful of all gods. Baal was the fertility god and was believed to enable the earth to produce crops and people to produce children. The worship of Baal included sensuality, involved ritualistic prostitution in the temples, and a human sacrifice such as the firstborn of the one making the sacrifice. Israel had turned away from God Almighty to the worship of Baal; it was pure idolatry. Ahab had temples erected and altars built to Baal all over Israel and led God's people to worship him. Jezebel was his wife and was the one who greatly helped, alongside Ahab, initiate Baal worship bringing hundreds of false prophets into Israel.

This is where and when God called Elijah to step into the biblical timeline. God has Elijah directly challenge the paganism by taking a stand and confronting Ahab. God was going to show to Israel that He is God, not Baal, by controlling the rainfall and sending a drought lasting three and half years and by Elijah's showdown on Mt. Carmel, calling fire from heaven to consume the sacrifice. God Almighty, by performing great miracles, would reveal Baal as a fake god and prove once and for all who is the true God. What is amazing here, is that Elijah's ministry was not an army, there are no allies to pull together, and no preparations to make; God simply selected Elijah to take the declaration of war to Ahab the king, which was God's judgment on Baal's followers.

God's Judgment on the Unrighteous Does Not Come without Provision for His Faithful

Riding the wave of God's purpose will rise and fall in our eyes. Because we are called to implement God's commands, consequences from our obedience will follow, which will produce waves to ride. We must be ready for them. God, many times, uses people to create the waves as He accomplishes His will on earth. This is what I call wave building.

Wave Building: Boldly Being Used of God

Wave building always begins with God using us to move with His purpose to accomplish His will. Over and over again, God chooses people to mount a major offensive to accomplish His specific task. Here Elijah is chosen to be that man. This means we must always be ready to speak as called by God!

We Must Always Be Prepared To Deliver a Word from the Lord

> And Elijah the Tishbite, of the inhabitants of Gilead, said to Ahab, "As the Lord God of Israel lives, before whom I stand, there shall not be dew nor rain these years, except at my word." (1 Kings 17:1)

These waves begin with Elijah being called of God to deliver a word of the Lord to King Ahab. Now, understand that Elijah to us is a nobody from nowhere. In other words, we know almost nothing about him. Here in the Scriptures, he bursts into the palace, somehow gets a face-to-face with the king who is trying to kill all of the prophets of God, and begins to deliver a direct word from God Almighty! Think about this for a moment. This king has converted to Baalism. He is seeking to kill all the prophets of God and rid Israel of any godly influence. Yet, Elijah stands in front of the king in full confidence and faith in the Lord God Almighty! How can he do this? Notice in the verse:

As the Lord God of Israel lives, before whom I stand. (1 Kings 17:1)

Only a person who had the experience of standing in the presence of his God before this moment could stand so boldly in the presence of the earthly king and deliver this message of judgment. Elijah was able to stand and face Ahab and proclaim truth and God's judgment because he had already been in the Lord's presence.

Before We Can Stand in the Face of Evil, We Must Stand in the Presence of God

Our confidence, boldness, and strength all flow from His presence. Today, there is a great need to stand against evil, but first we must stand before the Lord. Let me share with you a few examples of evil in our world today: compromise and complacency in the church, the holocaust of the unborn, the devastating assault against the family, the breakdown of godly marriage, and all sorts of other perversion and paganism. By many, evil is called good, and good is called evil. I believe God is looking for godly voices of fire to deliver His messages against the evil scourge in our land.

To be sure: *After standing in His presence, we can deliver His message with confidence and boldness.*

A voice of fire who will read His Word, believe His Word, pray His Word, and proclaim His Word, can expect God to move by faith. As a voice of fire, we are being called to deliver His message, so we prepare ourselves by standing in His presence.

Elijah stood in the presence of King Ahab and proclaimed God's judgment.

> There shall not be dew nor rain these years, except at my word. (1 Kings 17:1)

Why this judgment? Let's understand: Baal was called the god of fertility, believed to control seasons, their crops, and all the produce of the land. What better way to show the falseness of the god called Baal than to shut down what he represented? So, God's purpose was to call a voice of fire to deliver the judgment of God to the king of Israel that would strike at the heart of Baalism at its theological center.

Understand, this is a life-threatening judgment! God was not playing around here. Farms would fail, famine would strike the land, people would suffer, and even death would occur. So, this caused a major problem. Remember, Elijah was also there, living in the land. This judgment would impact him. So, God had a place designed for Elijah, a place where Elijah could both hide from Ahab and where God would provide for His servant.

Now, Elijah had built a wave of God's moving on Israel. This moves us to look at his riding this wave.

Wave Riding: Basking in His Provision

I think there are many times God calls and moves on behalf of His chosen voices of fire that create an amazing sense that we are right where He wants us to be, right in the center of His will. There is no greater place to reside than in knowing you are called, having accomplished His will, and you have pleased the almighty God! Sometimes, you might feel as though you are walking on air. You cry out, "Yes, God!" During this time, we are hitting on all cylinders with our communication, direction, and accomplishments as God has called us.

And for sure: *We can count on our God providing for us.*

> Then the word of the Lord came to him, saying, "Get away from here and turn eastward, and hide by the Brook Cherith, which flows into the Jordan. And it will be that you shall drink from the brook, and I have commanded the ravens to feed you there." So he went and did according to the word of the Lord, for he went and stayed by the Brook Cherith, which flows into the Jordan. The ravens brought him bread and meat in the morning, and bread and meat in the evening; and he drank from the brook. (1 Kings 17:2–6)

Elijah obeys the word of the Lord without question. He delivers the word of God to the king, and then what happens? God directs him to go to the place He has selected for him during the time of God's judgment. When we need to obey and deliver according to the Lord, God has our back, front, and sides! He will provide.

Our God Provides Our Physical Needs

God provided for Elijah's physical needs by both using the water of the Brook Cherith and miraculously feeding him meat and bread, morning and evening, by the ravens. Think about it. Ravens don't bake bread. God had other people in place to accomplish all of this to work. God is amazing!

Here we have Elijah, God's voice of fire, eating steak and bread and drinking from the brook. While the rest of Israel would be hungry and thirsty, suffering from the drought, Elijah had enough to eat and drink. When God sends us out to deliver His message, He will not abandon us. Elijah watched the provision of the Lord and the Lord's power over creation every day. Day-in and day-out, his needs were met, and he was right where God wanted Him. He ate and drank the menu planned and delivered by the God of miracles! Elijah is basking while riding the wave of God's provision. His wave included safety, quietness, cool water, the food God sent, and he was physically satisfied. But this is not all of God's provision.

Our God Provides Our Spiritual Needs

Elijah also enjoyed undisturbed communion with God. Where direct communication with God Almighty is, so is His purpose and wisdom. God's voice can be difficult to hear during the battle, but here, at the Brook Cherith, His voice was clear.

The Place of Obedience Is Where We Find the Voice of God

So he went and did according to the word of the Lord. (1 Kings 17:5)

Even though Elijah was alone at the brook, he couldn't tell anyone where he was because they might try to kill him. Elijah's faith increased as he saw his God provide and protect him daily. Many times, it's during our personal, alone times with God that our faith can greatly increase. Yes, even our greatest spiritual needs will be met. This is why our personal, private time with God is so very important. As we engage the Lord in prayer, pursuit, and obedience, what follows will be provision, protection, pathway, peace, understanding, and so much more.

At this point, it appears that Elijah has it made. God has made provision in a miraculous way, and Elijah was enjoying fellowship time with Him. He was riding the wave at the crest full of joy. But remember this: *Things never stay the same!* God is always working, and things can and do change radically. This is what I call wave breaking. The only way to go, is to ride the wave down.

Wave Breaking: The Brook Runs Dry

Even though God had provided all Elijah's needs, He also can cause a new direction in our lives. Many times, this will be through the circumstances that force a move.

This is the time to really listen carefully to the Lord because: *Our God, who provides, has the right to take away.*

> And it happened after a while that the brook dried up, because there had been no rain in the land. (1 Kings 17:7)

This provision was never meant to last forever; it was only a step in the journey for Elijah. Remember this fact: Elijah had prayed that it would not rain, he prophesied that it would not rain, and it didn't rain. So, his dilemma now with the brook drying up is an answer to his prayer. Not even Elijah could escape the effects of no rain. So, this begs the question, why would God place him beside a drying brook? This is such an important question that I would like to spend just a bit sharing.

Four Truths for When Our Brook Dries Up

1. The God Who Provides the Water Can Dry It Up

We often feel that once God gives us provision, He should never take it back. Once He gives us a spouse, a child, a parent, a business or a ministry, we really want it to be ours forever. And if or when He takes it back, somehow it seems that He has suddenly turned against us and is punishing us. Listen carefully: God is sovereign and has the right to give and to take away. Blessed be the name of the Lord. Elijah did nothing to create the brook provision, and he did nothing wrong for it to dry up. It was God's choice to allow this brook to dry up for Elijah, not anyone else's.

2. Our Dried-Up Provision Can Be the Result of Our Own Prayers

It was his God answering his prayer to stop the rain that resulted in the book drying up. This is like a wife praying for God to move in her husband, and then she must prepare or even expect to feel the effects of this prayer.

I believe that things like Christlikeness, maturity, patience, and humility usually come through a Brook Cherith kind of experience; it doesn't normally come from a weekend at the spa. Our most important journeys can be to the provisions that dried up over time. It pushes us to listen to God like never before; it doesn't allow us to get fat spiritually, and it prepares us to understand that the drying up of one provision will lead to something else God has for us.

3. Our Drying Up Brook Is Often a Sign of New Direction and God's Approval

Let's get this right. The Brook Cherith was provision and protection, not punishment for Elijah. However, he could not stay there forever; God had more work for him to do. The brook drying up was the Lord's way of saying it was time to move on, time to position himself for His next purpose for him. So, don't resist, fight, or give up. God is positioning us for the next work He has for us.

4. Through Unusual Provision, God Will Nourish Our Faith for His Future Plans

Before we can take on a task that requires spiritual strength for the future, our faith must be increased. This building up of our faith happens one step at a time! Understand: our Brook Cherith experience will increase our faith if we can see it! I have written a poem about the

Brook Cherith, and it is found in the back of the book. The end of this chapter would be a great time to stop, turn to it, and read it in the context of these truths.

A Brook Cherith experience can be very hard for us to go through. Many times, the command to be alone can be one of the most difficult for us to hear and obey. It requires us to stop our busyness, to get away from the spotlight, to cut out noise, and to still our minds to hear from God. You may feel like you are sitting beside a dried-up brook today. You can see the bottom of it, and you are praying that God would just bring more water, but He doesn't. It could be that you had a full bank account or a booming business, but the brook dried up. Maybe it was an exciting career or even a magnificent ministry, but the brook dried up. Perhaps a friend has grown indifferent and has left you high and dry with no promise of restoration—the brook dried up!

Hear this today: *Dried up brooks in no way cancel out God's providential plan.*

The reality is that our dried-up brooks cause God's plans to emerge. Our job is to have faith in Him and listen for His direction. It will come.

A voice of fire will embrace the brooks that dry up in our lives and look strongly to the Lord for direction. They will be willing to ride the waves of ministry as God gives and takes away! If you are willing to ride God's waves, I declare over you: *You will become a voice of fire!*

13

Persistence: Fan the Flame

YOU HAVE HEARD THE SAYING, "Actions speak louder than words." It is not if we have heard this saying, but rather, how many times have we heard it. Many times, we have shared this truth with our spouses, our children, and yes, even counseled our friends with this saying. But what about your spiritual life? What do your actions speak to God about you? What do your actions speak to you about your love for His church? Our actions, as Christians, speak much louder than our spiritual rhetoric. Especially to our Lord Jesus, our actions to His commands and revealed truth will speak volumes and speak more than anything to our zeal, passion and obedience. If we have a great desire to serve and obey our Lord, then we will follow this up with godly action within the context of family, friends, church and the world. In other words, by our actions others will see that we belong to Christ and our Father. Glory!

> Let your light so shine before men, that they may see your good works and glorify your Father in heaven. (Matt. 5:16)

This is not all that happens, which would be enough for sure. As we are serving faithfully and are found in obedience to our Lord's commands and will, we realize we have found ourselves right in the center of His will. And I find that there is no better place to find yourself as a Christian than in the center of His will! In fact, I like to call it in the center of the palm of His hand. Glory! This fans the flame of desire to please Him, serve Him more, and see His will be done on earth like never before. I can't emphasize enough the importance of allowing our actions to speak loudly for Christ, fanning the flame in our hearts for Him. James reminds us:

> But be doers of the word, and not hearers only, deceiving yourselves. For if anyone is a hearer of the word and not a doer, he is like a man observing his natural face in a mirror; for he observes himself, goes away, and immediately forgets what kind of man he was. But he who looks into the perfect law of liberty and continues in it, and is not a forgetful hearer but a doer of the work, this one will be blessed in what he does. (James 1:22–25)

Here we see a strong call to be found doers of the Word. In other words, we might say that actions speak louder than the tongue. The person who acts upon what they know to be truth will be blessed in what they do, not just in what they say. Also, we find in second chapter of James:

> What does it profit, my brethren, if someone says he has faith but does not have works? Can faith save him? If a brother or sister is naked and destitute of daily food, and one of you says to them, "Depart in peace, be warmed and filled," but you do not give them the things which are needed for the body, what does it profit? Thus also faith by itself, if it does not have works, is dead. (James 2:14–17)

Persistence: Fan the Flame

Again, James points to the idea that faith without action is dead. Yet, the converse must be true. Faith with action is so alive! This means that our Christian lives must be filled with godly actions for the Lord. A voice of fire will take godly action, and others will see that they belong to Christ and their flame for the Lord will be fanned to burn even brighter. This leads me to share what it will take to keep our flames burning brightly through godly actions.

Five Actions That Fan the Flame to Serve Him

> Then Saul arose from the ground, and when his eyes were opened he saw no one. But they led him by the hand and brought him into Damascus. And he was three days without sight, and neither ate nor drank. (Acts 9:8–9)

1. We Fan the Flame When We Obey

Then Saul arose from the ground . . . (Acts 9:8)

Paul (Saul) was told by Christ to go into the city of Damascus, and Paul got up and went! This is a very significant action of obedience by Paul. The Lord had commanded him to go to the very city to which he was already headed to persecute Christians and wait there for His instructions. Paul actually had letters from the synagogue leaders in the city authorizing his leading of violent attacks upon Christians. But now, after a personal encounter with Jesus Christ, his views of Christ had completely changed. He would no longer be pursuing his persecution mission but would be willing to obey Christ and go to Damascus with a complete and radical change in his heart, with a new desire to pursue this new relationship with the Lord. Instead of the proud Pharisee riding through the streets stirring fear in Christian's hearts, his entrance into the city was unimpressive to say the least. Instead of the proud Pharisee filled with hate and murder, he now was a blind, stricken man, trembling from his encounter with the King of Kings, groping for direction, and clinging to the hand of the one leading him. Now, this kind of obedient action didn't look spectacular to the world. In fact, as people found out about the man called Paul and his new helpless state, they probably said he got what he deserved. He would have looked ridiculous to the community at large and even the world. Understand this: the obedience of Paul was impressive to heaven and to Christ!

Obedience Speaks Loudly That Christ Is Our Master

This obedience spoke loudly to the Lord above that Paul's life was now different. It reminds us:

> Has the Lord as great delight in burnt offerings and sacrifices, as in obeying the voice of the Lord? Behold, to obey is better than sacrifice, and to heed than the fat of rams. (1 Sam. 15:22)

Obedience will fan the flame of our hearts with great confidence; God shall be pleased and shall reward those who obey!

2. We Fan the Flame When We Patiently Wait for the Lord

And he was three days without sight. (Acts 9:9)

After Paul (Saul) arrived in Damascus led by others, he stayed at Judas' home and had to wait for further instruction from the Lord. Here we have a type-A personality who is forced to sit still and wait on the Lord. This is not an easy thing for this type of personality. They like to get things done, to be on the move. There is no question that few things are harder than being still and waiting for the Lord. Remember, it was Christ who led him here in this condition. So, this is not a bad thing but rather exactly what Paul needed and Christ wanted.

There are few things more difficult than waiting for the Lord. I want you to notice something about the wait. There is a difference between waiting *for* the Lord and waiting *on* the Lord.

First, waiting on the Lord can be a time of great activity and accomplishment. This kind of wait would have suited Paul much better because of his personality. But this was not what kind of wait that Christ arranged.

Second, waiting for the Lord is a time of inactivity. It is a time that the soul cries out to be given direction in order to take action. These times of waiting for the Lord will reveal any rebellion within our hearts. These times are very important, for rebellion within needs to be addressed before the fire can be stoked into a brilliant flame!

This kind of waiting speaks loudly: *Waiting for the Lord speaks loudly of our dependency on Him.*

We see this issue in the Old Testament with King Saul who could not wait for the Lord, and it cost him his kingdom. Truth is, many will not wait for the Lord and on God's timing. Way too many today rush ahead of God at great cost.

> Wait for the Lord; Be strong and let your heart take courage; yes, wait for the Lord. (Ps. 27:14 ESV)

> Wait for the Lord and keep His way, And He will exalt you to inherit the land; When the wicked are cut off, you will see it. (Ps. 37:34 ESV)

A voice of fire will feed the flame of Christ in him through an obedient dependency on Him, waiting for the Lord!

3. We Fan the Flame When We Abstain

> Neither ate nor drank . . . (Acts 9:9)

This revelation of Christ on the road to Damascus and Paul's (Saul's) obedient response, now led Paul to know Him more. Paul began to fast, pray, and seek to understand Christ Jesus our Lord intimately. Paul thought he knew God, but after this amazing revelation, Paul realized he didn't know Him at all! So, Paul pursued Him with fasting from food and drink. Now, this is a serious fast. You can't live long without drink; you must have water to live. This tells us how intently Paul wanted to know Christ.

Abstaining Speaks Loudly That We Desire to Know Him More

Fasting and prayer should be a common practice of those who are spiritual and desire to know Him more. The early church fasted and prayed for sure, but it seems like today's church feasts and plays! The church today is dominated by the appetites of the flesh and plays more than prays! Oh that we as the church of the living God would simply focus our hearts and souls during a regular fasting and prayer event with the purpose of connecting and communicating with the Lord for His will to be engaged upon this earth. What an amazing move of God would be seen!

4. We Fan the Flame When We Pray

> Inquire at the house of Judas for one called Saul of Tarsus, for behold, he is praying. (Acts 9:11)

Paul was engaged in very private and very real prayer. This was a prayer that only God knew and saw. When God sees us in private prayer, it is real prayer indeed. Paul only had three days to live by abstaining from drink, so for him to live, God must take action. Get this: Paul is only going to depend on God, period. God immediately commanded Ananias to become the answer to Paul's prayers.

Real Praying Speaks Loudly of Real Conversion

My friends, private prayer can be more impactful than those prayed while others are with us. Private prayer does not try to impress anyone at all but is communicating only our heart's desires and concerns to our Lord. He sees and hears the prayers of the heart.

5. We Fan the Flame When We Learn

> And in a vision he has seen a man named Ananias coming in and putting his hand on him, so that he might receive his sight. (Acts 9:12)

True obedience places us in a position of learning. Christ had told Paul that he would learn more about what Christ wanted for him. Paul obeyed, and he learned more about Christ! It was a simple learning experience; Ananias would come to Paul, and Paul would get his eyesight back. Christ rewarded obedience to Him! Over and over again in the Scripture, we learn about His truth, that obedience controls our spiritual learning.

Learning Speaks Loudly of Our True Spirituality

Disobedience to Christ will leave you in the dark, and obedience to Him will bring your ability to see. Through your obedience, Christ will open your eyes to learn wonderful truths about Him and His ways. The truth is, no matter what you do, if you lack obedience, the fullness of the Scripture will not be open to you. However, if you follow in obedience, you will know Him on an ever increasing level, and His truth will be revealed all along the way.

> If you abide in My word, you are My disciples indeed. And you shall know the truth, and the truth shall make you free. (John 8:31–32)

As voices of fire, our actions should fan the flame created by our relationship in Christ. In fact, our actions must demonstrate that we not only belong to Christ, but we are passionately sold out to Him! It should reveal us as voices of fire. Fan the flame!

14

Conclusion

WE HAVE EXPLORED MUCH THROUGHOUT this book. I have expanded on topics that directly relate to becoming a voice of fire and to help enable in you a voice of impact. As you consider these truths and whether you will become a voice of fire, let me leave you with these guiding thoughts.

First, becoming a voice of fire has nothing to do with results. You may serve the Lord for years without what appears to be results in man's eyes, and that is just fine. For it is not man we seek to gain approval from or for man to judge our results. A voice of fire only faithfully obeys and leaves all the results up to God Almighty. This is a very difficult discipline to master. Voices of fire realize that there are forces we cannot see that are working against our every move. Therefore, man is not in a position to judge anything. Voices of fire must realize that we live in a results-driven society, and it seems that if we do not produce as men think we should, then we are not successful, or we're a failure or loser. Do not fall into this trap, for it is of the evil one.

This is just not so in the kingdom of God! Voices of fire are people who possess a view of being obedient to His call as their rock of service, understanding and acting according to His will, plan, and purpose. This is our biggest motivation and pleasure. A voice of fire understands that our God is a rewarder of those who diligently seek Him. All results of our ministry are in God's hand, period!

Second, as a voice of fire, you are what the world needs; so realize, our world needs you! The world really doesn't know this truth, but you do. Heaven has called you. The Lord has developed you. Stand firm and speak the truth in love but with conviction. Allow God to determine your voice according to His providential will. Your reward is not of this world. It is to come in great quantities when we see Him.

Third, God will use you to change lives! Yes, God will use you with all your weaknesses, challenges, and faults to impact lives beyond anything you can imagine. You shall be a voice of impact! Remember, only God can determine the impact you will have, but you shall have impact. Therefore, you nor anyone else can project what impact your voice shall have. So, it makes total sense to know Him, seek Him, and be a voice of fire for Him, and He shall use you to change lives. This is a principle of God. Obey Him and be used, period!

Fourth, you must not give up or be found a quitter! Quitting never got anything done, much less anything done for Christ. Our call is in spite of who we are as the world measures our every flaw, or how many mistakes we might make as some would point out, or how many times we think we fail. The real issue is our faith and how we view our call from God. Will our faith cry out to us: "I am a voice of fire, I shall be used of our Lord, I will not give up, I will not quit, I will not fail? For what God has begun in me, He shall complete!" If this is what you are made up of, I declare over you: *You will become a voice of fire!*

> "Answer me, O Lord, answer me, that this people may know that you, O Lord, are God, and that you have turned their hearts back." Then the fire of the Lord fell and consumed the burnt offering and the wood and the stones and the dust, and licked up the water that

was in the trench. And when all the people saw it, they fell on their faces and said, "The Lord, he is God; the Lord, he is God." (1 Kings 18:37–39 ESV)

I want to be this man today!

The Brook Cherith (ker'-ith)

Along our journey, across strange paths,
Bridged over by our works of the past,
Behind the caps of many years,
Beyond the pride and self-inflicted fears,
The Brook Cherith lies.

You cannot miss it, strive as you may,
As you travel on your way.
All faith paths that have been or shall be,
Through the Brook Cherith, passing is key.

Let all who come to this place bring
The purpose of Cherith Brook stream.

All those who journey, soon or late,
Must surely embrace this brook's fate,
And rest alone in solitude there,
Even battle with doubt, fear, and despair.
God pity those who cannot see,
Faith is tested when one with Thee.

Let all who come to this place bring
The purpose of Cherith Brook stream.

At His leading, placed by this brook,
To realize that He gave, and He took.
Lingering beside the brook now dry,
His refining fire burns and tries.
All to align our souls for His cure

Conclusion

That we may know Him more deeply for sure,
Shaping our lives, our faith to endure.
When our brook runs dry, then it seems
Time has come to now live the dream,
Faith-tested followers of our King!

Let all who come to this place bring
The purpose of Cherith Brook stream.

Based upon study of 1 Kings 17:1–7
Copyright Doyl Tully

Order Information

To order additional copies of this book, please visit
www.redemption-press.com.
Also available on Amazon.com and BarnesandNoble.com
Or by calling toll free 1-844-2REDEEM.

CPSIA information can be obtained
at www.ICGtesting.com
Printed in the USA
FFOW05n0243071017